MW00773642

Advance Praise for *That's Outrageous!*

"Fred Gray's writing is much like songwriter Sammy Cahn's descriptions of "The Second Time Around." The words are like a friendly home the second time you call. They speak of the comfort and solace of steady matured love; love that has weathered storms yet knows its own port."

Mary Stewart Adams,
Dark Skies Advocate and creator of the *Fairy Tale Moons* calendar

"I salute you for your gift of laughter, keen wit, and ability to throw caution to the wind and go for whatever you believe in. Your book is amazing, written from the heart."

Susan Manturuk,
who played a small part in Fred's literary journey
(see "Hair Loss" and "Long Tall Sally")

"Marvelous! A true revelation! From the funny and poignant opening profile of his brother Dave to the absolutely perfect last line of the book, this is a collection to be savored, cherished and admired. Every writer dreams of finding his ideal turf, the place or subject that will make his talent soar. Fred Gray has found his in the birch and huckleberries of his native Michigan—and we, his grateful readers, are all the richer for it."

Paul Chutkow,
author of an acclaimed biography of French actor Gerard Depardieu and
a memoir of Napa Valley pioneer winemaker Robert Mondavi

"Fred combines a little Mark Twain with a dash of Paul Harvey and Andy Rooney to bring alive everyday observations. Fred's common sense and great humor bring life to his stories. It's a writing style that I thought was long lost but lives on with Fred Gray. These are wonderful stories!"

David Crouse,
Emmy Award-winning documentary producer

"Fred Gray's grasp of the human condition is obvious, and his visceral sense of humor is never far from the surface; in conversation it emerges full bloom. If you love our language, are frustrated by its misuse by many 'professionals' in the print media, and cherish authors like Hemingway, reading That's Outrageous! will truly be a treat."

Richard Bidstrup,
Central American archaeologist, retired surveyor,
and long-time Emmet County Commissioner

THAT'S
OUTRAGEOUS!

A Gifted Journalist and Storyteller
Brings Heart and Humor to Life

Fred Gray

Flowing Well Publications
PETOSKEY, MICHIGAN

Books published by Flowing Well Publications are available at special discounts for bulk purchases in the United States by corporations, institutions, and other organizations. For more information, please contact the publisher.

FLOWING WELL PUBLICATIONS
P.O. BOX 485
PETOSKEY, MI 49770
(231) 487-0764

Gray, Fred, 1942-

That's outrageous!: a gifted journalist and storyteller brings heart and humor to life / Fred Gray. — Petoskey, Mich. : Flowing Well Publications, c2009.

p. ; cm.

ISBN: 978-0-9820670-0-0

1. Life—Humor. 2. Life skills—Humor. 3. Conduct of life—Humor. 4. American wit and humor. I. Title.

PN6231.L48 G73 2009   2008934960
818/.5402—dc22   0810

10 9 8 7 6 5 4 3 2 1

Cover and interior design by To The Point Solutions
www.tothepointsolutions.com

To Mom,
who led me, as a toddler, through the pine and birch
forests of Northern Michigan, to pick huckleberries
beside railroad tracks that are now but memories.

CONTENTS

Mom

Relationships

Youth

Politics

Predicaments

FOREWORD

by Ken Teysen

MANY MOONS AGO, I WAS THE THIRD MEMBER OF A very exclusive club in East Lansing. Its name, The Northeast Literary and Virgins Club, was derived in part from its location on the second floor of the Delta Chi fraternity house located at 101 Woodmere, just two blocks from the banks of the Red Cedar River. My roommates—Bill, a geologist, and Tex, a premed student—were the other two club members. Later they, respectively, became Dean of the Geology Department at Purdue University and a prominent Little Rock doctor.

As a break from our studies, we often would read aloud passages of poetry by Ogden Nash and Henry Wadsworth Longfellow, and stories by James Thurber, Mark Twain, and others. The topics were varied but dealt with everyday life and events. Some were serious but most were humorous. All had a keen insight on human nature and the subject at hand.

Since I was the only normal person (in my opinion), the idiosyncrasies of the other two were quite apparent. Bill was fastidious, neat, and orderly. In his world, there was a place for everything and everything in its place. Tex and I were quite the opposite, for we felt a messy desk and room were signs of a creative mind.

Tex also was a bookworm, and when reading was quite oblivious to the world. Periodically, when Bill could not stand the untidiness any longer, he would activate a voracious vacuum sweeper which swallowed single socks, vital notes, loose change, and anything else in its path. Many times he would tell Tex to lower his raised feet as that area had been thoroughly cleansed several minutes earlier. Tex also bought a new suit nearly every term; his definition of "being broke" meant he was down to his last ten dollars. We defined it as being without money. Period.

Still, our readings added much to our formal education. Without any doubt, the fourth member of our group would have been Fred Gray. He not only has an eye for the smallest detail of everyday happenings that some of us miss, he writes of them in a very compelling, tongue-in-cheek way. Talk about a raconteur (a name he once called me)! Fred is, indeed, one—Par Excellence! This term is not to be confused with *provocateur*.

On second thought, he might not have qualified for membership after all, as he was born only a couple of years after the Club was formed and his then incoherent babbling might have upstaged the rest of us—or caused us to drool a lot as we talked.

The many wondrous topics that Fred covers in this book are varied and wide-ranging and provide keen insight into these day-to-day events. It is indeed a refreshing delight from the constant doom and gloom presented daily by today's news media and numerous other printed opinions.

The world needs more Fred-type stories daily! I know that you, dear reader, will enjoy this book as much as I and will probably read it more than once.

Ken Teysen
August 2008

ACKNOWLEDGMENTS

I OWE MUCH TO MOM, NOW NINETY-FOUR YEARS OLD. She attended Wheaton College in Massachusetts and used her literary talents to great advantage for the Grand Rapids musical society. She found my essays interesting and amusing, even when she was the subject of a lighthearted jest or two.

Thank you to my siblings, Priscilla (Cilla) Laula, brothers Bill and David; and my children, Tallie and Ryan—all of whom stuck with me through thick and thin and were careful of preserving authentic memories of early family history.

Thank you to Uncle Charles and Aunt Marcia Bertsch, whose once-a-year visits to the Michigan north proved inspirational.

I owe a professional debt to my one-time Associated Press colleague and always close friend Paul Chutkow, author of acclaimed biographies of the French actor Gerard Depardieu and the late Napa Valley winemaker Robert Mondavi. After Paul read several of my early columns, he enthused that I had found "my voice." Not exactly sure what that meant for a writer, but having always wanted to perform with the Metropolitan Opera, I took it on faith that it was something to be treasured. Those two words have kept me going ever since.

I owe a debt of gratitude to the always spry and never-retiring members of the Mackinaw Area Historical Society, especially to the village's honored "gentle man" Ken Teysen, who was kind enough to write the Foreword for this book. As you will sense, Ken's wit and profound knowledge of the history of the area underpin every meeting and endeavor.

And, to Bill Marvin, the society's inventive publicist, who read my every column and commented favorably on them.

Thank you to Mary Stewart Adams, whom I consider Northern Michigan's brightest star in her wonderfully dark skies. She is a polished writer and an evocative speaker on all things celestial. Mary was kind enough to comment critically on a number of my columns prior to publication, thus saving them from catastrophe. I should add that Mary inspired several columns, including one about our insane trip across the Straits of Mackinac in our family's 1937 red canvas Old Town canoe.

I lift a frothy one to Susan, a friend and foil to my occasional arcane sense of humor. Susan deserves a niche in my Pantheon of literary sub-notables for submitting without complaint to my pranks. Fortunately for her, she later found relief, and perhaps retribution, in a suitable marriage elsewhere.

A toast to David Crouse, the journalist I mentioned in the Introduction, and his wife, Teresa—both inspirations to many.

And, thank you to:

The readers who had the good sense to restrain their critical faculties and occasionally effuse with joy to the author.

John and Debbie Rohe, my brilliant legal friends who have endeavored to maintain the earth as God meant it to be and keep the rest of us as honest as our human failings allow.

Journalist B. J. Hetler, who once let slip that she thought

me a poet, but gave me up in the end as an irredeemable hack.

Lyn Johnson, Administrator of Emmet County, who suggested I write a book; and to Kelley Atkins, his Director of Economic Development, who shares my outlook on many things, including trout fishing.

Jim Tamlyn, Chair of the County Board of Commissioners, who read my columns with the acute sensitivity of a long-serving politician.

Bonnie Nothoff, a dental hygienist and my political soul mate, who always found fodder for her campaigns.

Jan Stowe, a critic who wrote with interest about the several years she spent in Saudi Arabia as a nurse, and thus felt a certain kinship with me as a writer.

Engineer and road commissioner Dick Bidstrup, the most literate of public servants, who showered me with tributes, often scholarly crafted.

Keith Ogden, another literate road commissioner, who parsed my every sentence and phoned me often with the results.

Brian Gutowski, the Engineer-Manager of the County Road Commission, who wrote a fine and treasured tribute to me upon my retirement from the newspaper.

Fred Hoffmann, a local dentist and yes, a gifted road commissioner, who once called to say he found a column of mine the funniest thing he had ever read in a newspaper. (I should add he had a rather mordant appreciation of newspapers.)

Pat Harmon, another County Road Commission Manager, and commissioners Leroy Sumner, Frank Zulski Jr., Wayne Saunders, and Doug Way—all appreciative readers who drew laughter prior to meetings, often at my expense. To their credit, they consumed Michigan's "wild" food and invited me to share in the same.

County Clerk Jane Brannon, Irene Granger, and Deputy Clerk Cheri Browe, for their insight and scathing humor.

And, thank you to the publishers of the *Petoskey News-Review*, Ken Winter and later Doug Caldwell, for their encouragement and agreement to allow me to republish these columns, all of which first appeared in the newspaper.

And, thank you to Kendall Stanley, editor of the *Petoskey News-Review*, who, for better or for worse, touched nary a word of my copy from keyboard to the printed page.

INTRODUCTION

A T THE COUNTY FAIR THIS SUMMER, I BUMPED INTO David Crouse, a distinguished national journalist acquaintance of mine who was standing watch over the barn where his daughter's horse was being boarded. While the young elegantly dressed ladies rode in the dusty outdoor ring, David and I delved into our current ambitions, which included his work on a potential new film about Bobby Kennedy and my first, soon-to-be-published book—a collection of my favorite newspaper columns.

David, with five U.S. presidential interviews on DVD, enthused over my project, opining that my personal commentaries were of a type rarely written and would be treasured by future historians seeking a glimpse into the life of our times. Struck by the casual profundity of his remarks, I sought to repay him with a similar kindness. As it happened, I had just purchased several decades worth of Life magazines at a yard sale and recalled that the cover that struck me most was a portrait of Robert Kennedy at the time of his death. The photo turned out to have been taken by David's friend and colleague, Life photographer Bill Eppridge. I offered the magazine to David, and he avidly accepted.

This encounter was the highlight of the summer, and the thought expressed by David that my ramblings might have some significance beyond a pleasant sleep-inducing read prior to bedtime propelled me to new levels of confidence and exhilaration. After all, I had spent eight years anguishing over these twice-monthly meanderings, and finished my career at the paper uncertain of their value—beyond the welcome assurances of a small group of enthusiastic readers, among them my mother, siblings, and assorted relatives.

As you pour through the essays you will encounter moments memorable to the writer, at least. One you will not find, though it is perhaps the most remarkable, is about a woman who had read of the life and times of my devoted dog Rugby. She was moved to tears by the account of this small blonde retriever that so much wanted to live beyond his appointed time but was unable to persuade his hindquarters to follow. She left a message on my answering machine, apologizing for having had to recover from weeping before braving a phone call to me. (There can be no higher compliment from a reader to a writer.)

Several years later, on the day I retired from the newspaper, I crossed the street to give my respects to the postal clerks. Behind me in line was a woman who overheard my good-byes and introduced herself as the same devoted reader who had called in praise of the column on Rugby. Our eyes met and we shared a silent moment of delight and anguish. A chance encounter? Perhaps. But it was a perfect ending to a career of writing about serendipitous encounters.

Thinking back on the vicissitudes of my life, I find there were a few memories of early childhood that gave me constant direction, like the pole star to ancient navigators. The most vivid of these were of huckleberry picking with Mom, as giant steam locomotives lumbered beside us through the dense pine and birch forests of Northern Michigan. And clambering up the wet stone walls of the circular flowing well at Nipigon Resort on the Straits, to drink the purest, the most invigorating waters ever to spring from the earth. And then, from the screened-in cottage veranda, watching the silent freighters plow the waters before us, bound for far horizons.

Romantic. Searing. Forever evocative.

During those summers at the Straits, it was Mom and me, and Nanna and Grandpa, while Dad served far away in England and France as a physician in World War II. Later, there would be two brothers and a sister; and we fondly remember our times together in Northern Michigan.

Cilla lives in Charlotte, North Carolina, but owns a cottage on the Straits. Bill and his family live in Alanson, twenty-five miles south of the Mackinac Bridge; and brother Dave, a college professor, somehow misplaced in St. Louis, Missouri, dreams of sharing a year-round cottage with his big brother.

After a twenty-five-year career on the East Coast, a wonderful home and family in Connecticut, and several unhappy years in Colorado, I completed the circle and followed that pole star back to Northern Michigan, where I found a rewarding life awaiting me.

Much of that life is in this book. I wrote it for me—and for you.

I hope you enjoy it.

Family

MY BROTHER DAVE

BROTHER DAVE, THE PITTSBURGH HORNETS HOCKEY PLAYER of thirty-five years ago, who has since become a professor of international acclaim, was nearing life's sixtieth milestone and wasn't about to let anyone he knew within a continent of St. Louis miss it.

This included folks from Atlanta, Seattle, San Francisco, Charlotte, and Haiti, where brother Bill was completing one of his twice-yearly medical missions from Northern Michigan and was able to rebook his return flight to make the Saturday night gala. Just in time, as events would have it.

As if to assure himself an audience, Dave rented the west wing of Blueberry Hill, the landmark St. Louis bistro made famous by Fats Domino and the song of the same name, and by Chuck Berry, the duck-walking father of rock-and-roll who still performs there monthly.

Dave made sure Mom could perform at the grand piano, normally reserved for keyboard bashers, and checked out the Howdy Doody collectibles, Elvis souvenirs, vintage posters, lunch boxes, and fabulous old jukeboxes that line the bistro—to make sure all of us old folks would feel at home.

Hundreds of family, friends, students, and colleagues gathered near the Washington University campus for the weekend that marked three events—an engagement party for Dave's daughter, a celebration of his wife's tenure as associate professor at Fontbonne University, and the Big Birthday.

Family gathered at Dave's home Thursday night for a raucous recollection of growing up on the battlefields east of Grand Rapids, the site of abuse and torture Dave alleges he suffered at the hands of a merciless brother two years older than him.

That was me, by the way; and though I deny most of it, Dave has told the stories so many times he always wins the sympathy of his audience. Mom takes no sides, but shakes her head, as if to ask "Why me, oh Lord? What have I done wrong?"

Our children, now in their thirties, love the story hour— and to be honest, I never tire of the new cuts Dave makes from that colorful cloth.

When it comes to the part where Dave and I crawl out from our underground sand forts and together rout the invaders from over the grassy hill, flinging asbestos shingles that sail high as skeet and come darting down on our enemies, all pre-creating *Star Wars*, we stand together, united in triumph to this day!

The most amazing thing I learned about my brother during the weekend is that he cherishes the memory of the six weeks he dressed as a Pittsburgh Hornets hockey player, mainly to stop pucks for a team that folded not much later to make room for the expansion NHL Penguins. He wears his Hornets jersey today, as an emblem of pride, and attends St. Louis Blues hockey games where, his friends tell me, he becomes so vocally abusive that he is almost embarrassing to be around.

The second great moment of the weekend was at Blueberry Hill itself where, in front of hundreds chanting

"Happy Birthday," Dave rode in on an iBOT, a new-generation chariot for the disabled that rises up on two wheels to give the rider eye-level contact with those he meets.

This is a life-altering event for someone like Dave, a quadriplegic who has been bound to a standard wheelchair for thirty years and has had to look up to everyone he meets.

The iBOT, which Dave has been working on with inventor Dean Kamen and project underwriter Johnson & Johnson for almost a decade, also helps people who can't walk go up and down stairs and move through sand, rock, and gravel.

In addition to teaching at Washington University and traveling to Paris and Dublin and elsewhere, giving keynote addresses to conferences on disabilities, Dave now runs an evaluation and training center for the iBOT in a multi-state region.

"Every time someone gets up on the iBOT and is able to look eye-to-eye at their spouse or family member or friend, they all end up crying," Dave said, adding that even Mom, who has been through so much with Dave since his injury and miraculous spiritual rebirth, "got weak in the knees."

To me, the import of the hockey jersey is perhaps in its talismanic ability to invoke a moment of unencumbered bliss on ice, produced by the simple flick of a skate, something he can only imagine today in a body bereft of feeling.

Altogether it's a personal passion story for the season, one of suffering and redemption and renewal that inspires everyone who meets Dave, now face to face, eyeball-to-eyeball, and shares his spirit of uncompromising thirst for life.

CANOEING

MOM HAD WRITTEN OFTEN OF HER NORTHERN MICHIGAN experience, which centered on two distinct milestones. The first was her drive north with her parents and siblings in the summer of 1923 in an overstuffed Buick, to the site of a future cottage, about to be constructed at Point Nipigon-on-the-Straits Resort, nine miles east of Mackinaw City.

Mom was nine years old at the time and still remembers the two-day journey from Grand Rapids, including the series of sharp twists and turns on the gravel road between Mancelona and Kalkaska and the canvas tent over a wooden frame where the family spent the night in Traverse City.

The second water-parting event was the arrival of a sixteen-foot canvassed canoe from Old Town, Maine, which Grandpa purchased about 1937. Protected by a heavily oiled tarpaulin, the shiny red canoe survived decades of summers amid the snake grass and driftwood that lined Nipigon's sandy beaches.

At one point, before lake levels rose to the unimagined levels of the 1960s, we had the luxury of hoisting the canoe from the Straits using a wheeled lift stationed alongside a dock that jutted out from the base of the steep bluff in front of the cottage.

When the cottage was sold out of the family in the 1980s,

the fate of the canoe was uncertain. And, last year, we were forced to confront the financially painful decision of whether to allow it to continue to deteriorate or not. I polled Mom, two brothers and sister, and a bit to my surprise we all voted to have it restored at just about any price to preserve the legends of what was turning into an epoch.

We hired Mel Wilber, a retired carpenter, for the task. Mel worked on the canoe over the winter. In June, he, my brother Bill, nephew Zach, and I lifted the canoe from Mel's workbench to the carrier atop Bill's Yukon and drove it north to Wawatam Beach, just west of Mackinaw City, where we gave it a trial paddle on the placid waters of the Straits.

It was so heavy that even with the aid of my athletic nephew, Bill and I found ourselves gasping as we hauled the canoe to the beach, and privately despaired at the suffering of those who might again seek to romance the Straits in our canoe.

Sister Cilla and her husband, Sandy, on their annual July pilgrimage north and west from Charlotte, happily discovered the invention of a dolly with two balloon tires that turned the task of transporting the canoe into child's play.

Then came the ultimate test, both emotionally and physically, when brother Dave, the globe-trotting quadriplegic professor living in St. Louis, arrived with his wife, daughters, and new grandson, for a ten-day stay.

Dave and I had spoken of the possibility of giving him a ride in the canoe, but it struck me as a dream that both of us shared without believing it could ever be possible. Dave had an engineer friend who had invented a canoe seat for the disabled, but the engineer and I never caught up with each other in a prolonged phone chase.

But, Dave had an aide, a robust man in his early forties, whom I picked up at the airport and drove to the cottage. Mike had arrived from China the day before, so after three days catching up on his sleep, he agreed to help place Dave in the center of the canoe, buttressed by pillows and life jackets.

Margy, Dave's wife of forty years, and daughter Polly, helped while I stood by, worrying for all of us.

Mike took command of the canoe, while I sat in front, and together we paddled a great circle in front of Fort Michilimackinac, with Dave about as close to Heaven as he will get for many years.

When we returned to shore, there was Mom, clapping in delight.

"I suspect she was worrying for our entire outing, much like fifty years ago!" Dave wrote. "To be out on water, feeling the gentle push by the waves on the canoe and the surges when you two paddled, was so different than the feelings I have rolling over bumps, cracks and rock in my power wheelchair. Holding myself up, without a rigid back, side panel, and contoured seating was a physical challenge. When you guys paddled on the same side, the canoe dipped left or right. I was pretty sure we would tip over, but since the water was only two to three feet deep, I figured I'd just hold my breath until one of you turned me right side up!"

Brother Bill is a sentimentalist at heart, like the rest of us. He recalled that the canoe symbolized the "wonderful summers when we had no responsibilities! The smell of the canoe reminds me of the cottage and the attic, and brings back summers at Point Nipigon."

And sister Cilla?

"The minute I saw it," she wrote, "I was flooded with memories of Nipigon, the cottage, the flag pole, the view across the Straits, Grandpa, the dock, and that funny contraption that raised and lowered the canoe . . .

"I'm not sure I went on many excursions in it, but it was integral to our time at the cottage and those feelings of summer—of openness, adventure, possibility, fun and freedom."

We memorialized our feelings for the canoe, for each other, and for the epoch we call Nipigon by purchasing a family plot at the Mackinaw City cemetery. We hope it will be years before we meet there, under the lilacs and birch trees.

But we are determined to meet again, and forever. We still have a lot of canoeing to do.

CLOSING THE COTTAGE

His servant picked up the spade and dug a grave long enough for Pakhom to lie in, and buried him in it. Six feet from his head to his heels was all he needed.
Leo Tolstoy, "How Much Land Does A Man Need?"

IT HAD BEEN ON MY MIND EVER SINCE MOM RETURNED TO Charlotte for the winter. So, I spent a couple of hours closing down her cottage last weekend. I had to steel myself to the annual ritual, a melancholy ordeal filled with reminders of another summer spent in close friendship that had been nurtured through a lifetime of filial devotion and shared interests.

As I approached Mackinaw City, the maples and oak and birch of the surrounding forests were rapidly turning to pumpkin, russet, and burgundy—the ephemeral colors of an undulating quilt that would briefly hug the earth before disappearing in sodden layers of parchment brown.

I was alone as I turned onto the single lane that led to her cottage—alone but for the chill wind that whipped off the churning Straits and rushed through the deserted lanes of Wawatam Beach, demanding obeisance from the towering pines that bowed and scraped before it.

Mom's cottage stood as witness to a life whose best moments had been spent with family in Northern Michigan, sharing treasures hidden under protective boughs of birch and pine. Hers was a modest structure and a step down from the spacious family compound built in 1924 and sold to strangers only several years ago. Some of Mom's best, and wealthier, friends shunned the replacement dwelling, observing that the tidy bungalow lacked the aura of the Nipigon retreat.

But for her, and the rest of the family, this cottage was ideal and somewhat like a second marriage: unpretentious, comfortable, and undemanding. She had difficulty with her friends' complaints, but she philosophized along the lines of Leo Tolstoy, who asked: "How much land does a man need?"

The answer, in both cases, turned out to be, "Not much."

There were the two yellow flower boxes under the windows that had to be emptied of potting soil that had nourished the cheery red and white blossoms through the summer months.

And there were the green plastic chairs that had to be dragged down the ramp that had been built for brother Dave, and then gently nested in the shed that I had freshened with a coat of paint not so long ago.

I fed the birds and squirrels and chipmunks one last time, filling the clear hanging cylinder with sunflower seeds and assorted grain, and scattering several handfuls of the mixture over the ground beneath as a parting gift to the wingless critters that scampered about. After all, the separate gatherings of cardinals and woodpeckers and blue jays, interrupted by lively troupes of earthbound creatures, had been our favorite entertainment at the natural dinner theater outside her window.

I ran a damp cloth over the dining table, where Mom had served her biweekly cornbread-stuffed whitefish and baked squash dinners, occasionally spiced by a tomato aspic salad or a bowl of fresh fruit.

I dropped the blinds over the windows and closed the slats to protect the floral fabrics from sunlight that would otherwise cause them to fade.

And I picked up the books of Broadway piano music that Mom used for inspiration, and which I occasionally pored through, avoiding anything with more than two flats or one sharp in my labored attempts at re-creating the sounds of music.

Then I spotted the to-do list we had ambitiously put together on Mom's arrival in June, and reviewed it with apprehension. Still remaining for next year:

Remove moss growth from shed (ten years in progress)

Remove tree stump (postponed for a second year)

Recycle newspapers (and dispose of my articles?)

Visit Celia (Mom's homebound college classmate)

Good, I thought. Leaving a few things for the next season somehow assures us that there will be a next season. There has to be one. The natural continuity of life demands it.

BROTHERHOOD

I'VE BEEN FASCINATED BY AIRPORTS EVER SINCE MY FIRST flight in the early 1950s, from the homely stucco terminal in the Grand Rapids outback to the even homelier Pellston Airport shack that rested on a one-time potato field. That one-hour flight, in the first row window seat of a Capital Airlines DC-3, earned me my captain's wings at the age twelve.

A couple of years later, brother Dave and I, less than two years apart in age, hiked a dozen miles to the Grand Rapids Airport, without a penny in our pockets, to temporarily escape the double whipping from Dad that was sure to follow our friendly altercation of the day before.

Granted, we had only used household weapons of choice—mine was a hammer and, although I have forgotten Dave's, I guarantee it would have been lethal in the wrong hands. But, the following day, we willingly set aside our ongoing battles for a few hours respite before the inevitable consequence.

As the older brother, one who crafted balsa and rice-paper model airplanes as a hobby, the airport was a natural destination. The sight of a burgundy and silver DC-3 rolling along the tarmac transported me to exotic places that the flying carpets of storybooks would do for others.

After an hour or so of peering at the metallic bird through the chain-link fence, we hiked back home, detouring through the rolling fields of summer after a passing motorist advised us that Dad had called out the state police in an area-wide search for his wayward sons.

"You had better get home, fast, if you know what's good for you," he said before speeding away.

As we scrambled over the sandy rise opposite our home, we spotted Mom and Dad on the porch in high dudgeon, awaiting our return. Neither so much as twitched. Dad appeared forebodingly grim, his eyes fixed on the horizon; Mom seemed endearingly anxious.

As I recall the moment, I imagine them posing for Grant Wood's *American Gothic* portrait of a decidedly mirthless couple awaiting their kids' return from . . . where else? The airport! Wood took some liberties, of course, like substituting a pitchfork for Dad's hairbrush, but either implement would have made the point.

And yes, Dave and I paid dearly for our unauthorized journey.

But, despite the painful end, our hike to the airport and back was worth it. For in one brief day we forged a bond of brotherhood that has lasted a lifetime.

THE FLAG

DURING THOSE BRIEF LIMPID MOMENTS JUST AFTER dawn, when the straits lay still in the crisp pine air and Bob-lo Island seemed a few skips of a flat stone away, Grandpa Bertsch would hug the triangular bundle to his chest and grasp for the latch on the screen door, find it, and gently push it forward, taking care not to make any unnecessary sound.

Under the watchful elephant-eye window above, he would carefully step to the tufted earth and move in slow thoughtful steps to the tall white-washed pole among the birches and next to a low spreading cedar bush, which I knew to be the home of a family of large and dreaded garter snakes.

It was a private moment for Grandpa and the flag, and occasionally, if my brother and I were awake, he would invite us with a whisper to join him and share in the brief and simple ceremony of raising the spangled banner as God would have wanted it, in the thrall of daily re-creation.

Back home in Grand Rapids, Grandpa was an old-world businessman, a pillar of the Methodist church, a graying usher who every Sunday escorted the faithful to their usual seats, a man Nanna dragged against his will to the weekly bridge party, a man whose sole enjoyed diversion seemed to be listening to "Oh How I Hate to Get Up in the Morning," on his Victrola, well beyond the machine's useful age.

Yet here, in the unvaulted chamber of the Michigan north, was my quiet, gentle grandfather in somber reverence with a symbol that, as I look back, revealed the essence of the inner man, a dutiful man driven not by flamboyance or ostentation, but by belief in an idea somehow captured in a rectangular piece of tri-colored cloth.

As boys on the cusp of adolescence, my brother and I shared the ritual of a secret order, without a word, as we attached the flag's grommets to the clothesline that looped through a pulley far above, and under Grandpa's somber watch, drew the flag aloft in measured paces.

The three of us stood, eyes fixed to the flag as it swung slowly around the pole far above us, in a moment of silent prayer before retreating back, to a day of summer pleasures in the birch and pine forests.

I would like to think that Grandpa had it right when he chose to display the flag in a private manner; thoughtful, dutiful, and reverent.

The rules for displaying the flag, the whens and hows intended to foster respect, are well and good. But, they cannot instill true respect for our flag; we can only encourage it by example, as many of us were fortunate to have had and will pass along to our children, or by education, as a second choice.

I'd like to believe that had Grandpa Bertsch been asked to give words to his thoughts on one of those mid-century mornings, among the pines and birches, next to the spreading cedar shrub full of garter snakes, he might have said, "Boys. Here's what I'm thinking. We're all Americans. That's our inalienable birthright, our most precious possession. We don't need to prove it to each other. Let's move beyond the ostentatious show of pride and move forward, individually with humility and thoughtful search for continuous national renewal. That will light the path to the answers to the challenges we face.

"That's the message I believe in, and am trying to impart to you during the time we spend together with our flag, and it's why we raise it every morning and secure it on the mantle every night."

EMAIL FROM SOUTHEAST ASIA

Dad,
I leave the 24th and will be officially in Thailand the
25th of June. Thanks again for storing the pictures.
Hopefully, you will enjoy them.
                    Love, Ryan

I LAST SAW RYAN AT MY NIECE'S WEDDING IN ST. LOUIS SEVERAL months ago. My son was about to turn thirty and looked fiddle fit.

Ryan lives in Vail, Colorado, where he teaches school; skis with ethereal grace; and coaches soccer, his spring and fall passion. Unlike me, he has a healthy head of hair and a wiry athletic body, which he uses to his advantage and to my anxiety. He lives on the edge, at times quite literally.

While attending the University of Colorado several years earlier, Ryan and a Norwegian friend—without a word to us—decided to ski down a backcountry glacier in Rocky Mountain National Park, more than ten miles from the nearest two-track. It was late August and they wanted to get an early start on the ski season.

That evening, my daughter, Tallie, suddenly appeared at our table at The Rapids restaurant in our tiny town of Grand Lake, and earnestly whispered with obvious distress that

Ryan was fine. "We shouldn't worry," she said, "although we might want to visit him at the Granby Clinic.

"Just a few scratches," she assured us. "Not to worry."

We leapt from the table and made the fifteen-mile trip in record time, to find Ryan on a gurney, his wrist broken and his skin bloody and abraded. He looked as though he had fallen into a crevasse, which it turns out, he had.

Although a hiker had spotted the would-be skiers in distress and radioed for help, high winds made it impossible for a helicopter to attempt a rescue and they had to limp their way back to civilization.

Thus, when Ryan informed me during the June wedding festivities that he was about to leave for Southeast Asia for ten weeks of hiking and rafting, I felt a surge of that all-too-familiar anxiety.

He had made a deal with his school's principal to pay for part of the trip in exchange for a series of lectures upon his return.

I tried to disguise my apprehension; but here was my only son about to risk his life in the very part of the world that I was fortunate enough to avoid during the terrible years. (The word *Vietnam* conjures images of death, horror, and devastation to me, as I'm sure it does to all Americans of my generation, particularly those who experienced it first-hand.)

But instead of an M-16 rifle or a canister of napalm, Ryan carried a laptop and digital camera, sending me photos and narratives of his adventures whenever he found a phone. His first email could have been straight from the crevasse:

Dad,

Well, I officially turned 30, and it was quite memorable. I took a bus from Bangkok to Chiang Mai for a whopping $3.75. I unfortunately got what I paid for. The ad said there would be air conditioning, a *movie and comfortable space. Unfortunately, they went 0 for 3 on their promises.*

At 10:30 a.m. we broke down in the middle of nowhere, and a Thai family sold us drinks and food. (The bus was actually not that bad, but it was made for really small people!) We think the bus had brake problems, but it got us to Chiang Mai.

My Swedish friends on the bus were very sweet—they wrote me a nice letter and gave me chocolate-covered almonds for my birthday. I also cracked open a large beer at midnight and reflected on my best time of the last ten years.

Through the following weeks Ryan regaled me electronically with accounts and pictures of his mountain treks and river trips through the backcountry of Thailand, Vietnam, Laos, and Cambodia. Here's another taste from my mountaineer/adventurer son:

From there, we hiked another two hours to ride elephants through the jungle. Since I was the smallest guy, I got to ride its neck, which was both scary (at first) and exhilarating. I can now see why it took Alexander the Great so long to try to cross the Alps!

At another point, he told me of the warmth of the Vietnamese he met:

Amazingly enough, they hold NO grudge. As a matter of fact, when I tell them I am American, they smile broadly and shake my hand. They do so because the U.S. offers economic stability and a lifestyle that many look up to. The Vietnamese are some of the kindest people I have ever met, and I feel safer here than in many places in the United States.

Engrossing reading, to be sure, especially for a father who lived through the summer in dread. Still, the most welcome snippet from his summer journal was the single sentence he tacked onto a particularly hair-raising account:

From here, I will go back to Bangkok and maybe visit the beach for a few days of relaxation before Cambodia.

Once a father, always a father, I suppose.

Ryan has just returned home, safe and sound and full of tales of adventure and thoughtful insights into the cultures he stumbled upon, accounts that should endear him to his fortunate students in Vail.

As for me, I'm hoping for another family wedding soon, for the opportunity to hear him out on the many questions I have about how old generations caught in the maelstrom years can heal, and how their progeny are able to live without bitterness toward my son or the other occasional Americans they meet.

The miracle of generational renewal works for us as well: it took a son to remove his father's scabs.

THE WEDDING

IT SEEMS THAT YOUNG DAVID ENTERED THIS WORLD PER-
forming a triple gainer before slicing gracefully into the
deep end of the gene pool, where years before I was
barely getting my feet wet at the other end.

As recounted by my brother David at his son's wedding
in Seattle last weekend, this child prodigy, at the age of five,
grew impatient when his father could not immediately set
the Lionel train right after an accident.

"Fic it, daddy," he demanded.

But, unable to wait on one half of his gene source for a
solution, young David began reading electrical circuit books
to solve the multitude of problems that came his way. Thereafter he was able to say, with some pride, "I fic't it, Daddy."

He fic't the train and, a few years later, Microsoft, too; and
retired at the age of thirty-something, to take up ballroom
dancing with wasp-waisted ballerinas.

In the interim, Big David fell off a roof trying to cover the
hole left in his roof by a cement mason, broke his neck, and
ended up a quadriplegic, restricted forever to those few
places wheelchairs are free to roam.

During the ensuing years, young David cared for his father,
as did his siblings, Beth and Polly, and his gifted and beautiful mother, Margy, the other half of the genetic source code.

While other boys his age led normal lives of assorted pranks and misdemeanors, young David helped his father regain his life, spirit, and profession. Whatever he lost in childhood pleasures, he gained in insight, empathy, and resolve.

Big David showed his son and the rest of the world incredible fortitude, prospering beyond hope despite his fate. In less than ten years after his injury, he was appointed by President Reagan to the position of Director of the National Institute of Disability and Rehabilitation research. There he directed federal research dollars to the study of treatments and environmental changes that help people with disabilities participate fully in family and community activities, a civil right described in the Americans on Disabilities Act.

Today, brother Dave is an associate professor at Washington University in St. Louis, traveling in his wheelchair throughout the world, speaking on the problems of the disabled, the most significant one finding someone to help him through his daily rituals that you and I go through in five minutes.

After his success, young David, not one to forget the love he enjoyed from his parents, invited them to join him on a trip to Florence and Rome, Margy's lifelong dream. Though he would have loved to join them, brother Dave demurred, knowing that taking care of a severely disabled person was no way for young David and Margy to enjoy Italy.

Last year, young David found someone he thought he loved, or as he told his father, "Someone he KNEW he loved," a woman born of another world, whose parents, of Chinese ancestry, had been caught up in the Vietnamese maelstrom and eventually emigrated to Texas.

To help celebrate their triumph, young David and his fiancée, My Ton, invited their families and progeny to Seattle, where their ancestral worlds merged in subtle, complex, and separate ceremonies.

The Eastern ritual was three pages long, and Big David and Margy were asked to wait in their "house," an adjoining hotel room, while My's father and mother presided over a ceremony that included a family crest, incense, a roast suckling pig, and a family tree rooted in a thousand years of fascinating history.

The bride and groom and their entourage then proceeded to David and Margy's "house," where they were introduced to the Gray and Esterline families in front of their "ancestors' table," highlighted by photographs of family forebears I hadn't seen for years. Among them was a photo of Mom, whom I had to leave in Michigan; for though her heart was with us, at eighty-eight, she didn't have the stamina to make the exhausting trip.

My daughter, Tallie, an Ingrid Bergman look-alike, with large soulful blue eyes and radiant blonde hair, arrived from Colorado with her two-year-old son, Bo, who fell into a primal catlike crouch whenever he spotted a bird fluttering through the damp Seattle air. I hadn't seen either since Bo was born.

I had never met Margy's brother Albert, a double- Ph.D., who flew in from Greensboro, North Carolina, where he professed computer science. The attraction to the groom and his professional interests might seem obvious, but his real interest turned out to be the roast pig.

Albert had grown up on a Minnesota farm, where pigs were raised for slaughter, and he asked me if I thought it would be rude if he swiped the head of the sacrifice, a delicacy he had been denied for years. I suggested he wait for a decent interval, which he did, but in the end he got his wish.

The conclusion of the three-day affair was held at The Ruins, a seemingly abandoned warehouse that turned out to be the secret haunt of the city's well-to-do. Inside, the drab cement blocks were transformed into an Italian villa, with faux flowers adorning the walls and a tropical paradise of real flora jutting from urns scattered throughout the richly appointed rooms.

Brother David spoke with humor and feeling of his memories of the Lionel train child turned groom. Then Margy, her russet curls cascading over an elegant crème-colored dress, took the floor with humble grace. As she spoke eloquently of her marriage, and the tests of love and commitment that went with it, she left no soul untouched.

I glanced over the linen table, across and through the fluted glasses that sparkled in the candlelight, to Tallie, who was profoundly affected by Margy's words. Tallie's eyes were huge and wet with emotion and her face was streaked with tears. Was she feeling joy for the young couple who had found one another, something that had eluded her and her parents despite storybook beginnings, or was she weeping for the romance of Margy and brother Dave, which had triumphed over the most heart-wrenching adversity?

I couldn't bring myself to ask.

Life

ADVICE FROM BIG AL

C HANGE MAKES LIFE INTERESTING, AS I CAN ATTEST. IT
was a humid August day in the early 1980s when the
Newspaper Guild declared a strike by several hundred Reuters' news staff—the first job action ever by
employees of the venerable news agency.

Quite honestly, I was hardly persuaded that the promise
of a few cents in additional benefits was worth the impending
pain; but, as I was a point at issue—management insisted my
job be exempt from guild jurisdiction—I had the good sense
to keep mum and take my medicine. (Medicine and donuts
turned out to be the keys to survival.)

Here I was, living in a house beyond our means in a plush
Connecticut suburb of New York City, and the mortgage had
to be paid and two kids fed. I was at the tail end of a generation that equated manliness with bread-winning, so I pored
through the *New York Times*, looking for alternative employment. I couldn't bring myself to ask my wife to help make
up for my shortcomings, and she wasn't about to volunteer.

In the classified section several notices beckoned at me:
"Taxi Drivers Wanted."

Well, I figured I had given my fingers a workout for the
past ten years, not to mention my brain, so it was time to
give my feet some exercise. After all, they knew gas pedals
from clutches and brakes.

I had little choice but to respond to the only ad that didn't ask for experienced drivers. I took a series of trains and subways to Long Island City which, at the time, was a desolate wasteland along the East River. Eventually I found the address barked at me over the phone. It had been a gas station many years before and was now almost completely hidden by weeds and debris. The entrance had been unused for ages, but a fading red arrow pointed me to a side door which yielded to a quick twist of the hand and a sharp thrust of the shoulder.

Inside was a dark vaulted chamber with 25-watt light bulbs dangling from a spider web of wires. The only guy around asked what I wanted. When I responded, he pointed to an enclosure made of plywood sheets extending outward from the corner of the dank and filthy building. The word "Office" was scrawled on a sheet of cardboard.

The boss, Big Al, was aptly named, if apes have names. Al was at least six-six and wore dark-green eyeshades wedged over a bald head that could have doubled as your prototypical nuclear warhead. He wore wide suspenders over a greasy flannel shirt and smoked cheap cigars.

In your face, pal.

I was more than a bit squeamish since it was immediately clear Big Al didn't suffer fools kindly, and I was clearly a fool.

I advised Big Al, politely, that I was responding to his ad, and mumbled assurances that I could be counted on, come hell or high water. My ability to handle breaking news stories with skill and grace just didn't register.

Big Al rose sluggishly from his dull leather throne and peered at me from under his shades, sizing me up. Or should I say down, given his perspective? Then he chomped on the wet stub of his unlit cigar and jabbed at me with a tobacco-stained forefinger. "Gray," he said. "I can tell that you're a . . . NICE GUY." He spit it out, as though it was the absolute

30

worst thing he could say about me. Then he rolled his eyes to the ceiling in Zero Mostel fashion and shouted, almost in apoplexy, "You can't be a NICE GUY and be a TAXI DRIVER!"

He let that sink in for a moment. Then, in case I didn't get it, he offered an explanation that began in a whisper. "Little old lady has a sack of groceries. She asks you to carry them to her apartment. "And YOU, BEING A NICE GUY, you LEAVE THE CAB and DO IT!" he shrieked, the sweat flying from his forehead, his hands flapping through the air. I actually thought the warhead was about to go off.

"You can't leave the cab to deliver groceries for little old ladies OR ANYONE ELSE! No. But you're a NICE GUY, Gray, and you'd DO IT!"

The sarcasm hung in the stale air. I was certain my trip had been in vain. We'd have to give up the house, I decided.

In desperation I tried to convince Big Al I really wasn't such a nice guy after all. I considered revealing some of my worst habits. Slighting comments about my mother-in-law? Would that qualify? But, I really couldn't think of anything that might satisfy Big Al's blood lust.

"I promise you, I'll never deliver a sack of groceries for a little old lady, or any one else," I said, timidly.

Big Al just shook his head. Why he gave me the job, I'll never know. He must have been desperate. I drove the night shift for three weeks, perched on an inflated rubber donut to ease the pain of the unmentionables as I negotiated the potholes of Manhattan.

Made a lot of friends, too. Delivered no groceries; but dispensed a lot of good advice. So good, in fact, that a pair of former fares—two women from Miami—made their way up to my office after I returned to work, this time as a manager, to thank me for my recommendation on a favorite Thai restaurant.

ESCAPE FROM STEAMBOAT

THE BLUSH WAS OFF THE ROSE FOR THOSE OF US LIVING downstairs in Steamboat Springs, Colorado. To be sure, it wasn't all dismal. There were chummy Sunday barbecues, the buoyant surround of dazzling wildflowers, minty sagebrush tumbling along the parched outback, and spruce-covered mountains that peaked out in melting snow at more than 10,000 feet.

Sun-burnished streams of liquid copper meandered through a wilderness so desolate that my idea of a perfect summer day was to throw on the saddle and ride far from Steamboat—in my blue Ford Explorer—to a point where no radio station would register on the car's electronics. I found it a hundred miles away, where south Wyoming tapped into eastern Utah just north and west of Colorado.

"Hole in the Wall Gang Country," read one ad. "For those who wondered what Butch Cassidy and the Sundance Kid was all about." It embellished:

> "It's about fine horses, their powerful strides, and their thundering hoof beats, carrying you up, through the sagebrush, breezing by scrub cedar trees, eating dust from your riding companions (unless you're riding in front). You see an eagle circling above, and deer and antelope running down the gaping draws."

I was working for a daily newspaper in Steamboat, under

an editor who too often recalled his finest days as a military policeman (MP). In my off-hours, I helped run a crafts shop, put together by my talented former wife, who also fashioned herself a military policeman. The high turnover rate of staff at the paper was evidence of how the MP's regime was regarded. I was becoming very senior—after six months of active duty. The publisher was so proud of our work, she gave the paper away and still—presumably—made a bundle.

I had thought that after thirty-five years of working for news agencies in New York City and taking early retirement, it would be illuminating to see the world from the basement up, a change from the 49th floor down.

At the paper I wrote about the Black Widow murderess who lived in town, in between taking good care of eleven husbands. They made a movie of her exploits and I have the video, which I cherish. I shudder to think I might have been next had I the means to attract her. A wild conceit!

I wrote about historic characters, most of them treacherous, and on the other side interviewed the 10th Army (Mountain) Division's Gene Hames, who with several dozen GIs took command of Mussolini's villa on Lake Garda hours after the Italian dictator and his mistress fled to their fate near the end of World War II.

And I wrote a column about what I called "Times Square West," for the dozens of signs that sprouted up in what otherwise would have been a beautiful campsite. In it, I recounted how I had traipsed through the trailhead with my twenty-six-year-old son, Ryan, both of us bound in aluminum showshoes. We passed a sign advising us that "No Motor Vehicles" were allowed on this stretch. "Initially, I found this intriguing," I wrote, "because thirty feet up the path was another sign limiting one's speed to 15 mph. Let's see, I thought, I can't legally be in a motor vehicle but I am allowed, somehow, to move at a rate of 15 miles an hour.

That's absolutely no problem if I'm on foot, and probably even less so if I'm on a bike. But then, not far away is another sign announcing that 25 miles per hour is okay from that point forward, or backwards." I asked myself if I'd I fallen into the same hole that Alice did, to reach Wonderland.

Out of curiosity, I asked Ryan why he hadn't brought his eight-month-old black lab Pele. After all, black labs are synonymous with Steamboat and what could be more perfect than a brief outing to the town's landmark with our favorite town mascot? "Oh, he barked for the first time last night," Ryan replied, absent-mindedly, cryptically.

So what? I thought to myself. Dogs are born to bark. A million years of genetics have controlling interest here. Just then we passed a sign that read: "Barking Dog and Leash Laws Enforced."

"I see," I mused. But, before I could decide whether to congratulate my son for being an upright law-abiding citizen or chastise him for being a wimp, we approached a second sign advising us, pictorially, that this was really a cat crossing, and pleading explicitly, "No Dogs Please."

So, when I drove to my old stomping grounds in Mackinaw City for my one-week vacation, I checked in with Mom. At some point, I bought a copy of the *News-Review*. Tucked inside was an ad for a reporter. I checked in with Managing Editor Ken Stanley and a few weeks later, after returning to Colorado, Editor Ken Winter called with an offer I couldn't refuse.

It was a sweet day, saying good-bye to Mark, the displaced MP. He caught me in the parking lot and almost bit my head off with disgust. He had such plans for me, he said. I had really let him down.

And so, I raise a glass of Colorado spirits to the Kens for lifting me out of that beautiful morass and back to this, the playground of my youth and a land of comparative sanity that most of you have enjoyed for years.

HAIR LOSS

In Penny Lane there is a barber showing photographs
Of every head he's had the pleasure to have known.
from "Penny Lane" by The Beatles

THERE IS NO SUBJECT BEYOND COMMENT FOR WAYNE, THE
garrulous barber of Howard Street, who gracefully
rounded seventy a year or two ago.

Wayne, a weekend kayaker in season, spotted my head
out of a multitude of reflective domes at the Two Hearted
River Campground on Lake Superior last summer, and
rushed over to introduce himself to my friend Susan.

"I'm Fred's barber," Wayne gushed with undisguised
pride, giving me a once-over from top down and clapping
me on the back. I was clearly overdue, but Wayne had the
good grace not to breathe a hint of it.

Despite Wayne's valiant efforts, I'm not much to look at;
but that moment at the Two Hearted was special to me. It
meant I was not just another head in his gallery, or if I was,
he had a special spot in his heart for every one of us. Like the
barber of Penny Lane, Wayne likes showing off every head
he's had the pleasure to have known.

I like Wayne for many other reasons though—his droll stories, his almost bedside manner, and for the pleasure he gives others, especially my family, when he returns me to civilization once every two months or so.

But, I especially enjoy his forthright answers to the searching questions that languish in my mind, such as: "Have you ever come across someone who has actually benefited from a hair restoration product, such as the one that plays a starring role on the Rush Limbaugh Show?"

"Never once in my fifty years of cutting hair," Wayne said with a gentle laugh. He went on to tell me of the occasional fellow who is certain he has sprouted new growth following dedicated applications of the latest scalp fertilizer.

Wayne said they often refuse to return when, after careful inspection and with his credibility on the line, he responds to a cautious inquiry with something like: "Well, no. I can't honestly say I've seen that much change since your last visit"—which may have been six months ago.

So, every time Rush suspends his engaging commentary to give much too much time to the Excellence in Broadcasting Network's shameless profit center, I picture him glancing at his comb-over visage reflected in the golden EIB microphone and pondering the question posed at least hourly on his airway: "Is your hair thinning? Then why haven't you tried Avacor?"

It is one of the few questions to which Rush has yet to respond.

WILD BLUEBERRIES OF PARADISE

THIS YEAR'S MID-AUGUST VACATION BEGAN AUSPICIOUSLY enough. For starters, there was the traditional visit to Shirley Clark, co-owner/baker of the Berry Patch in Paradise, where the cognoscenti of the North indulge in her heaven-sent wild blueberry pie à la mode. So bubbly is Shirley about her lard-crust pies that she'll tell you of the dentist from Ohio who drives up to her shop on Lake Superior every year at Christmas to pick up twenty pies as Yuletide gifts for his best patients.

His best patients? Almost unbelievable in this day and age, isn't it? Visions of million-dollar lawsuits flit through my head, like fat globules racing through your arteries. But, I believe her.

So delicious are these flaky gold-and-blue wedges, usually afloat in thick dollops of melting ice cream, that Margy, my discerning sister-in-law from St. Louis, rated finding and tasting them her Number One adventure whilst visiting relatives at the family cottage on the Straits in July.

I've actually seen grown men, many of them overgrown, come into the shop, plop down, and demand a piece of blueberry pie, fearing they may have been shut out for the day. They fidget in uncertainty until they are served, then turn into the proverbial milk of human kindness—and even begin conversations with their wives!

My August respite usually includes rolling and picking in the abundant blueberry bushes in the centuries-old graveyard just south of Whitefish Point. But this year, there was not a drop of blue to be found on the ground. "No rain, pure and simple," Shirley said sadly, when I told her. I was devastated, stealing a glance at my empty five-gallon blue-and-white enamel pail that I had collected from the cottage in a moment of brainless optimism.

Trust but verify, I thought, as I drove to the usually lush blueberry fields along the Two Hearted River that spills through towering sand dunes into Lake Superior. Again, nothing. My final proof was the backup blueberry picker who sells me berries when I'm short of bragging rights. The young man said he had only apple pies to sell this year, even though I spotted the same hand-lettered "Blueberries" sign at the edge of the highway.

Shirley said she bought enough blueberries at the end of last summer to carry her though pie season this year. "But," she said, "the real pinch will come next summer."

When my brother Dave called to remind me that Margy's birthday was coming up, I thought how nice it would be to send Margy one of Shirley's pies. I called Shirley, who warned me that shipping pies is bad business in the summer heat (think exploding pies.). "However, late fall would be perfect," she said. "I'll check shipping rates for you and call you back."

Sure enough, she called me back. "One pie overnight goes for $32.50. Can you believe it?" Shirley said in deep gloom. That brought the price of a $12 pie to nearly $45, with shipping, to St. Louis. So, I sent Margy a card with a lame blueberry joke on it.

Not much, I thought, but just wait till next year!

I asked Shirley to save us a pie, no matter how lousy the season. "After all," I reminded her, "we're no longer strangers in Paradise."

CHRISTMAS TRAVEL

Over the river and through the woods . . .
on an aerial sleigh.

MANY OF YOU DO IT AND SUCCEED. FOR YOU, I OFFER my sympathy and congratulations. For those who do not, I'll give you a flavor of what it is like to experience holiday air travel, to savor around your family fireplaces.

Christmas is a time to share with family and friends; for me that meant flights to and from Charlotte, North Carolina, to visit Mom and my sister.

It also meant enduring a month of uncertainty as to whether the turboprop would actually take off from Pellston Regional Airport in the heavy snows I was sure would fall that weekend. I had a three-day window for the trip and could not afford a missed flight or connection. Everything had to jibe. I knew I was taking a big chance.

I closely monitored the weather reports as D-Day approached. The flight was scheduled to depart at 4:40 p.m. on Friday, December 22. I left Petoskey for the airport about 3:00 p.m. in a flight-threatening snow flurry that was topping off six inches of white road cover left by the previous night's storm. When I arrived at the airport an hour before flight time, I took advantage of a prime reason for using the Pellston airport—free parking. The long-term lot was over half full, with dozens of permanent "residents" covered with thick blankets of snow—an indication to me that seasonal visitors were taking advantage of what I suspected was free over-winter parking.

On the departure board, a freshly cut blank piece of cardboard had been inserted to the right of my flight, in the slot reserved for the usual white-on-red designations "on time," "delayed," or "cancelled." As there were several of the latter two posted against other flights, you can imagine my imaginings of where my plane might be.

The explanation was simply that the plane had been delayed a bit but could make up time and actually arrive and depart on time. Apparently the predicament didn't readily lend itself to the available inserts, so the blank announcing nothing at all was created. Very creative. Very disconcerting.

It then occurred to me that the very best Christmas present for my family would be a fresh slab or two of Lake Michigan whitefish; but I calculated I didn't have time to make the round-trip to Mackinaw City to pick it up. So, I selfishly decided to treat myself to a fish dinner at the Brass Rail Restaurant in the airport. I figured it would at least be real food and fortify me for my four-hour layover at Detroit Metro. I was right.

Once at Metro, I was treated to a seemingly endless round of gate swapping, and shortly before flight-time joined a line of fellow passengers trying to enter the D17 ramp, the one posted on terminal screens for the Charlotte flight—even though the scrolling red dots at the gate itself spelled "Philadelphia."

To everyone's confusion, the gate had, indeed, been held for the delayed flight to Philadelphia. On inquiry, we were told the Charlotte flight had been changed to C16, whatever the departure screens said. "Didn't we know?" the gate attendant asked in annoyance.

When we raced the quarter-mile to C16—with five minutes left before the scheduled departure—we were confronted with a sign that informed us D16 was the gate for the flight to Saginaw. The attendant, a bit put out that we should question her, assured us this was really the flight to Charlotte and was about to leave. "We had best get aboard immediately," she said.

Exasperated and with a leap of faith, we clambered aboard the aircraft, closed our eyes, prayed, and ended up in Charlotte, a city without a trace of snow, and only a half hour late.

On reflection, it's a wonder that any traveler bound for Charlotte, Saginaw, or Philadelphia—or their checked luggage—actually ended up at their rightful destinations.

The return trip, on the evening of Christmas Day, was a comparative delight. The flight from Detroit Metro to Pellston was overbooked and overweight, and there were several hours of uncertainty for most of us, including a family of three who had sugarplums dancing in their heads of free flights to anywhere in the United States, Mexico, or points elsewhere.

Unfortunately for them, the free flight went to a single fellow who was promised a seat on the first plane out the next morning—although it seems that flight was also overbooked. (I didn't stick around to find out whether he was going to make it back.)

Our flight took off on time and we arrived in Pellston ten minutes early. More than a foot of fresh snow had piled on my car during my three-day journey, but brushing it off was a welcome price to pay for having completed a successful holiday travel experience.

ICE FISHING

A Three-Day Journey Through Hell

MY CHILDHOOD BUDDY RAY, WHOM I HADN'T SEEN IN thirty-five years, convinced me that by following US 2 west, I would eventually reach Duluth, from where a thirty-mile drive north would bring me to his Finnish-style chalet on the edge of the big lake. Superior that is. It was long past time for a reunion, and Ray, with his chipper nonchalance, averred that Duluth was only six hours away from me, "Tops."

Moments before I left the office on Friday, my colleagues assured me I was looking at ten hours, on a good day. As it turned out, it was a bad day and they were wildly optimistic.

Undaunted and unknowing, I packed up my 1994 Ford Explorer and set off for points north and west, to become one of four grumpy old men taking part in Ray's annual First Day Festival on opening day of ice-fishing on Minnesota's inland lakes.

At nine the following morning, I knocked on the cabin door and was greeted by three very brilliant, and very hungover, university professors, one retired and two active. Dale had flown in from retirement in Albuquerque, while Mike and Ray had driven up from Minneapolis.

The three had mercifully been through the fish wars before, and were returning for more. I was encouraged.

Ray outfitted me with oversized galoshes, and I recovered a stretchable pair of my daughter's leotards and a beanie-sized ski hat from the backseat jumble of my car. The rest was standard issue.

We drove our cars inland for an hour, stopping at a state park where we unloaded two plastic sleds from Mike's black pickup. Dale and Mike took the early shift in harness, dragging the sleds along a packed snow path leading half a mile to the lake.

It was a tough hike, but nothing compared to what I will always consider the ultimate punishment for hubris. Here was a small lake, peppered with fish shanties and covered with a deceptive cloak of white over a thick layer of icy slush.

Ray insisted on pushing through to the far side, where fishing had historically (for them) been the best. And so, when we encountered the icy swamp we marshaled though.

Then Ray, seeing I was experiencing some difficulty, tossed me a pair of grossly undersized snowshoes from the sled, suggesting they might make things easier. I strapped them on, hoping to glide across the crust of snow to our destination. Instead, my snowshoes plunged through the snow crust to the hard ice below. In between were eighteen inches of slush that promptly filled my boots.

Leaning over to free myself, I plunged headfirst into the chilly brew. In the moment of shock that followed, I imagined myself eye to eye with a wary trout, asking me, "Who's catching whom, sport?"

Too proud to admit discomfort, I dragged my sopping self to the nether shore, where the boys were twirling their augurs and cutting holes through the ice. "How are you doing?" they asked cheerfully. Were they blind?

In the four hours that followed, we caught two trout, each

close to twelve inches. I "caught" mine while my back was turned, drilling yet another hole in the ice in exasperation. Ray, suddenly observant, noticed my bobber was depressed and yanked on the line. I took over for the final three seconds and landed the trophy myself.

After sundown, we returned to our cars, this time taking the frozen trail around the edge of the lake. Once in the cabin, I filled a red plastic pail directly from the hot water tank and sank my feet into the mineral bath. Bliss, I thought.

Just then, Ray traipsed by and spotted the steam rolling skyward from my footbath. "Gawd," he exclaimed. "We use that bucket for DRINKING WATER!" That's when I officially became a grumpy old man.

The journey to Hell is paved with good intentions—and about six inches of packed snow.

GAMES:
THE SPICE OR SLICE OF LIFE?

The games we play with others can last a lifetime.
Like chess. Or almost a lifetime. Like Scrabble.

MORE SOBER IN MY OLD AGE, I HAVE REPLACED TRYING to reform the world by settling for a good game of Scrabble, wherever I can find one. I figure, if I lose, I have only myself to blame, or my opponent to praise. What could be nobler or more selfless?

Although Mom and I can't wait to dust off the old Scrabble board whenever we get together, she spends the winter in North Carolina; so I prepared myself for a Scrabbleless winter in my new home in Northern Michigan.

My newcomer's advertisement, designed to lure the locals into a friendly game of Scrabble, went unnoticed, until a curious and daring librarian of some skill invited me to match wits. Ah ha! I thought. Another tilt at the windmill of words.

Since then, barely a week goes by without a few delicious games. She is ahead, some thirteen games to ten, scoring high in the 300s, drawing Q's and U's with annoying regularity, and dropping the Q on triple letter squares with alacrity.

When I draw a Q, I'm usually stuck with it through the game, its ten points to be deducted from my final score and added to hers. So be it. The luck of the draw, I console myself as I leave for home.

I'll simply have to learn to mind my P's and Q's a bit better, and honor a one-pointed U with the respect it deserves. Even if it's only worth a single point, it has the potential for combining with another letter to provide a game-winning masterpiece. Or master pieces, if you will.

Such humiliation! Such adventure!

And, here's the kicker: Her children—self-confident teenagers all—scorn the game as one for losers, old fogies, or worse. But, as soon as we break out the board and draw our letters, these same children silently pull their chairs to the table and intently check Mom's rack of tiles against the dictionary with a view to finding the winning word. They occasionally rise to the challenge, and gloat in their new-found treasure.

It's become a challenge for the ages, and one I hope they'll not soon forget!

ELEGANT BARBS

FOR ME, ONE OF THE MOST DEVASTATINGLY FUNNY LINES of all time came midway through *Murder on the Orient Express*, when the overdressed and overwrought Lauren Bacall was fomenting to Inspector Poirot. Bold and brassy, Bacall pushed herself up against the eccentric Belgian sleuth with the gusto of a ballplayer challenging an umpire over a called strike three. "Don't you agree the man must have entered my compartment to gain access to Mr. Ratchett?" she demanded, alluding to the murder victim next door.

Sitting across the aisle, Wendy Hiller, as the veiled-in-black Russian dowager Princess Dragomiroff, without looking up from her knitting, responded dryly, "I can think of no other reason, Madame."

It was the perfect squelch, this elegant barb, and one I return to time and again, waiting for my turn to invoke it.

A famous line, yes, but second only to my Nanna's line of forty years ago, when she and my parents visited our apartment along the Huron River in Ann Arbor. It was Dad's birthday and my wife wanted to treat him to a cake he would never forget. She somehow discovered he adored caramel cake and frosting, so she prepared a three-layer version that had the dimensions of a very short, very thin stack of pancakes. Potato pancakes.

She tried to make up for the cake's shortcomings by lavishly swirling caramel frosting to such creative peaks that when it was served, the frosting dropped off in gobs, revealing the stiff cardboard layers inside.

Members of my side of the family were tempted to laughter; but out of respect for the tender feelings of my wife, they glanced furtively at each other and then braved the concoction in funereal silence.

Nanna, who was the ultimate in grace and correctness, finally broke the hush with a tenuous, if solicitous, "Perhaps, dear, you left out the liquid ingredient."

At the time, we were so stunned by the gallows humor of Nanna's observation that no one so much as snickered. Years later, it has become our favorite memory of our family matriarch.

I recently received an elegant barb for trying to bluff my way to gastronomic fame through a recipe given me in reciprocity for serving an authentic Borscht Moscovskaya to the entire *News-Review* staff.

It was the occasion of a going-away party for publisher/editor Ken Winters, and Ken was most gracious in accepting a bowl of the beet soup with sour cream and fresh dill, and later the recipe. Those brave enough to taste the concoction loved it, or said they did, and accepted the recipe when I offered it to them hours later.

So, when Hilary offered me a recipe for Solyanka, an accompaniment to borscht that was taken from the vegetarian *Moosewood Cookbook*, I ran off to buy the ingredients, which included a half cup of sunflower seeds.

As directed, I sprinkled the seeds over the casserole, baked it, and then sliced a generous portion to share with Hilary in thanks for her attention to my culinary education. Hilary took one look and burst out in laughter, refusing to touch the dish. She gently noted that I had taken the instructions too literally, and used whole sunflower seeds (of the farmyard variety), not the edible shelled ones.

The result was that while the casserole likely appealed to birds, it certainly did not tantalize any one of our species who doesn't relish pulling the shards of seed covers from between their teeth with each bite.

When I returned from assignment an hour later, I found a bag of shelled sunflower seeds on my desk. It was an elegant, if unspoken, barb—and one I richly deserved.

I have since offered the casserole to my fine-feathered friends, who were very appreciative, have returned for seconds, and sing its praises.

APPLE CIDER

A PPLE GROWER JOHN KILCHERMAN CONSIDERS APPLES TO be gifts from God. So do I; especially when pressed. And until a few days ago, I considered the making of fresh pure autumn cider to be a lost art, lost to the imperatives of the health community that watches over our well-being with near Puritanical solicitude.

I had been told that the sale of unpasteurized cider was made illegal in Michigan, as well as in most of the United States, after the outbreaks of e coli associated with cider in California, Japan, Scotland, and elsewhere in the late 1990s.

Believing that to be so, I picked up a half-gallon of cider bearing a label that assured me it had not only been pasteurized, but also contained potassium sorbate and sodium benzoate as preservatives.

When I returned home, I uncapped the jug, held my nose, and sipped the cloudy liquid within. It was, predictably, awful—mindful of sludge in a service shop.

I thought it ironic that one can smoke cigarettes, at least in open air. You pay $5 a pack for the privilege of killing yourself (and arguably others), slowly but legally. But—you can't drink unadulterated cider. Huh?

Why not simply require a label, warning of the consequences of drinking unpasteurized cider, and let it go at that? As we do on menus for undercooked meat, or for that matter, eggs.

I've been reliably told that no life has ever been lost in Michigan to cider, and relatively few elsewhere.

I considered the cider constraint to be a breaking straw, so outrageous I toyed with the idea of joining the Libertarian Party. Or escaping to Canada to find a glass of the unadulterated beverage. After all, some very pungent memories were held in the balance.

I decided to try the latter alternative first.

We drove north, crossing the U.S.-Canadian border at Sault Ste. Marie, and dropped in at the provincial government's tourism information center. There an amiable young lady, when asked for directions to a local farm market or other source of cider, suggested hesitantly we might be able find one on St. Joseph's Island about an hour east. Not a bad guess, considering her brochures described the island as "still very rural in character."

We stopped at several markets and on the island itself, confounded clerks with questions about cider. Amazingly, the product was unknown to them. One suggested that we ask Mennonites at their farms. We did and were met with blank stares.

Returning to Petoskey, our hometown, I was determined to press my point. I started with Jim Cranney of the U.S. Apple Association, a lobbying group based in Washington D.C. Jim told me he sympathized with my view, and in fact had made the same arguments to the Food and Drug Administration for ten years before changing his mind on the subject.

"For a long time, we took the position that as long as our industry utilized apples picked from the tree and handled them properly, and processed them in a sanitary environment, it's probably perfectly safe," he said.

"However, in the environment we're in these days, with

the prevalence of e coli and virulence, we can't count on everyone following these practices."

"Most importantly for me," Cranney said, "the FDA exempts retailers who make their own cider from its regulation requiring pasteurization." He said they only have to affix a warning label. I later confirmed that the State of Michigan had done nothing to pre-empt the FDA ruling.

Cranney said there are differing methods of pasteurization, some of them resulting in poor quality cider but others so effective that the average consumer can't tell the difference between the treated and the non-treated.

He said that with the latter, differences in taste are more attributable to the variety of apples and methods used to make the cider. He said preservatives help shelf life and maintain quality for a longer period of time, but he admitted that they definitely affect the taste of cider.

I confirmed all of this with Richard Friske of Friske's Orchards and with the Michigan Apple Committee.

Friske makes cider with and without preservatives for wholesale from Traverse City to Mackinaw City, as well for retail at Friske's Market on US 31 at Atwood. Denise Yockey, executive director of the Michigan Apple Committee, told me there are 112 cider makers licensed by Michigan Department of Agriculture, and at least half of them do not pasteurize the cider made at their own mills. "All are inspected each year, and their cider is tested. No outbreak of food-borne illness has ever been linked to cider in the state of Michigan, which speaks well of the people making cider."

If you have similar appetites as I do, you can find an orchard that sells fresh unpasteurized cider, free of preservatives, by visiting www.michiganapples.com and navigating to "consumers" and "farm markets." You may have to make a few phone calls to nail it down.

Cheers!

"LONG TALL SALLY"

MY COMPANION AND I SPENT A SUNDAY AFTERNOON driving home through a howling storm, listening to the maniacal ramblings of America's most original rock-n-roll artist and trying our best to unscramble such lyrics as "She's biffa specie ga."

Susan earned my everlasting respect for picking out "You won't do your sister's will," the very first time "Lucille" went sailing by. After all, I had waited fifty years and listened to hundreds of recitations, trying to in vain translate the phrase.

Every time I heard the lyric, and others equally obscure, it was as if I had overheard some sonic screech caught in one of the gigantic radio telescopes that record the pulsation of the universe in the event that someone out there was trying to communicate with us. The futility of trying to divine the secrets of another world—to come so close as to almost touch the mystery and yet be rebuffed by it each and every time—was enough to drive me mad.

Let me say, in hopes of redeeming myself among you traditionalists, I have spent equal time listening to Modest Moussorgsky's own portraits in sound, "Pictures at an Exhibition," trying to imagine a trashy hut built on giant chicken legs.

But here, on that rainy afternoon, we had Little Richard on the other end of our solar microphone, ranting about a "Long Tall Sally" who was so biffa specia ga that when Uncle John saw Aunt Mary coming he ducked back in the alley.

Susan's lifelong endeavor—helping the blind learn to see through word pictures delicately drawn—had been exceptional training for the task at hand. Yet she too was nonplused at more than one of Little Richard's sound bites.

For days, I imagined that Susan and I were alone in the mystery. I had never seen a headline announcing the discovery of the meaning of "biffa specie ga," although there were undoubtedly millions of devoted fans who had searched for it.

Later, I went to our own radio telescope—Google—where I discovered that such intelligent earthlings as Richard Corliss, a senior writer at *Time* magazine, had been similarly perplexed by the phrase.

"And what language!" Corliss wrote. "Ten years earlier a boy might have sat reverently by the living-room Zenith to hear the Metropolitan Opera and pick up a little Italian along the way. Now he hid in his bedroom with his plastic 45-r.p.m. player straining to figure out what the heck Little Richard was screaming, 'Well long tall Sally she's biffaspeesheega . . .'"

I felt both redeemed that others found themselves in the same quandary as Susan and I, and a bit saddened that someone else had been there before us.

Before I reveal what Corliss discovered, let me say that comparing the dozens of versions of lyrics to Little Richard masterpieces, those that appear on the Internet, is a bit like the old game of "telephone." To take single example, Little Richard's most famous hit, "Long Tall Sally," one listener heard that Uncle John "claims he has the misery but he's havin' a lot of fun," while another decoded it as "He claims he hasn't missed her . . ." Others found after careful listening that Sally was bald-headed, or boll-headed, or bold-headed, or ball-headed, or even blonde-headed.

I also learned that Richard supposedly wrote the lyrics while working as a dishwasher at a bus station in Macon, Georgia, and titled the song "The Thing" before settling on the name we all know. If true, this could help explain everything—or nothing.

Early in their career, the Beatles thought "Long Tall Sally" worthy of imitation, but cleaned up the phrase "bald-headed Sally" to "long tall Sally" before changing it back to "bald-headed Sally" in their final recording.

And by the way, Richard Corliss finally concluded, rightly I believe, that "she biffa specie ga" is best rendered: "she's built for speed, she's got . . . (everything that Uncle John need.)"

After all my self-doubt and investigation, I can understand and empathize with Corliss, who wrote with an eloquence I envy:

"If I were older, I might have thought these artists pretentious or inane; if younger, pretentious and primitive. Finding them at exactly the moment when my sensibility was ripe for shaping is my blessing and my curse. Without doing much but enjoying them then, and without hardly thinking about it since, I let them set the bar for my critical standards.

"Those standards must still apply, for when I replay 'Long Tall Sally' . . . for the dozenth time or flip through a precious old Mad *comic, I am still enthralled—and convinced that, when I was a kid, I had excellent taste, and surer of my enthusiasms then than I am now."*

Well, Richard, both big and Little, let's just say we inhabit the same world, or is it the same universe?

"YOU GOT GAS?"

I WAS DRIVING NORTH TO MACKINAW CITY THE OTHER DAY, and the roads were treacherous with ice. So it was with relief that I stopped at a lonely convenience store along the way, slid inside, poured myself a cup of stale coffee, and picked up a newspaper to gather my nerves for another foray into the elements.

As I was about to dish out my $1.50, the young gum-chewing woman behind the counter looked up at me and asked, "You got gas?"

I was stunned by her audacity.

I admit was scanning the headlines and was not quite with it, but as my subconscious checked out the Rolaids display in front of her, several responses flitted through my mind.

"No, do you?" was the first I considered, but thought it a bit flippant.

"Does it really show?" I asked myself, running through the list of usual symptoms.

I ended up with, "No, but thanks for asking."

She laughed, probably thinking me a fool. I had entered by a side door, intent on buying coffee and a newspaper and skedaddling. It didn't occur to me that this mid-route oasis was also a gas station.

I realized it's an innocent question asked of all convenience store customers these days, in hopes of forestalling a drive-away.

But it reminded me of a good friend who told me that while interning as a plastic surgeon with the Army years ago, he would occasionally suggest to a stranger in the elevator that he could do wonders with the bearer's prominent nose if given the opportunity. It was a shameless, assertive promotion—and of questionable taste—but you could consider it a bit of free consultation and a way to earn a little extra money.

And, dear Lord, who are we to deny a man an honest living?

SERENDIPITOUS ENCOUNTERS

ANY WRITER WORTH HIS STIPEND OF SALT IS WELL ADVISED to worship at the shrine of serendipity, where a chance encounter may have pleasant consequences worth contemplating, and even writing about. Serendipity is what distinguishes a blind date arranged by an earnest friend, from a chance encounter with the girl of your dreams over a lost contact lens on a windy morning in front of St. Patrick's Cathedral in New York City.

That happened to me early on in life, when contacts were made of hard plastic and occasionally lost with a rapid flexing of the eyelids. The girl of my dreams spotted me on my knees, groping the sidewalk for that clear speck of plastic and, apparently out of sympathy, joined in the silent search. Alas, she found the lens and I lost the contact, as she disappeared with a beguiling smile into the multitude. I would have preferred it the other way around, but the lesson was quickly learned: one must seize the moment, even in adversity!

So, thirty-five years later, when a reader, let's call her Anna, sent me a note of appreciation for a column I had written, I responded with alacrity. After all, being an occasional columnist is a lonesome occupation, and infrequent compliments should be acknowledged and even encouraged.

In the exchange of letters that followed, Anna, in her mid-fifties and living near Frankfort west of Traverse City, led me down a fascinating path that eventually turned to reminiscences of her father and my mother, both pianists of talent.

Anna's father had given voice to silent films as a means of putting himself through school, while a decade later Mom played after-dinner music for her college classmates.

Half a century later, Anna moved in with her widowed father and his Vose baby grand piano and Rogers Trio theatre organ, which he played for hours in daily reverie until his death several years ago. After he died, Anna had no idea what to do with the organ, so she called the Music House museum in Acme, several miles north of Traverse City.

"They came down to play it and inspect it, and the younger man who came to play it caressed the keys with a hushed intake of breath like something wonderful was happening," Anna wrote.

"The older man told me then that they had been looking for a Rogers Trio for several years, so that the musicians who played the antique instruments would have something on which to practice. It was a match! And I thrill to think of Dad's organ still being played daily."

Anna still had her father's piano and, as the Music House is one of my favorite attractions in Northern Michigan, I sent Anna a copy of a column I had written over a year ago following a visit there, in part to set the stage for the home performance I knew was fated to come.

Mom, now eighty-eight, was about to leave Northern Michigan for her annual trek to warmer climes; but, before departing, she planned an afternoon visit to a friend in Arcadia. It had dawned on me that Arcadia was not far from the Vose in the Woods and with the stars and moon in favorable alignment, Mom could bring Anna's piano to life once more.

Anna welcomed the idea. When Mom and I arrived at the

appointed hour, we approached Anna's house amid sounds of an instrument in torture. Anna was clearly determined to return her piano to its former glory of song and spirit.

After a friendly greeting and slice of zucchini bread, Anna invited Mom into the music room, where the polished Vose rested proudly, its cover propped up to allow the sound to flow, and stacks of yellowed sheet music were neatly piled about. Mom sat on the bench, ran a few arpeggios up and down the keyboard, and broke into a lively rendition of "Sweet Georgia Brown" and a more tentative "September Song."

Anna listened, her thoughts somewhere else, perhaps in another world.

The next day Anna sent me a copy of the note she had forwarded to her friends:

"There was a very special treat for me this weekend. Happy chance brought a lovely lady here on Sunday afternoon to play the piano. She is of Dad's era and ilk, and the piano happily responded to her loving touch and joyfully brought forth music of the style I thought never to hear again.

"She graciously played for at least a half hour, and brought back a lifetime of memories, as well as deep appreciation for her talent.

"All too soon, she was off to her summer home near the tip of the mitt, leaving me filled with gratitude and admiration for the funny little turns in life that have the ability to bring us so much joy!!"

Those few tuneful moments on an otherwise quiet afternoon were, as Anna said, the fruits of serendipity: the funny little turns in life.

NEW THOUGHTS, OLD QUESTION

IT WAS APRIL 9, 1970, WHEN UNITED AUTO WORKERS LEADER Walter Reuther's Learjet broke through clouds, hit trees, and burst into flames while attempting to land at Pellston Airport. As the new boy at AP in Detroit, it fell to me to fly north on that stormy night, strapped into a leased twin-engine cargo plane as we careened northward through a flashing midnight sky on my first extraordinary assignment. The weather was too uncertain to allow us to land at Pellston, so we continued north to St. Ignace, where I engaged a taxi and drove south to the scene of the crash.

Half an hour later, with notebook in hand, I dictated two paragraphs to veteran AP labor reporter Pete Mahan before he said, "That's fine, young man. Now, get yourself back here."

When I returned to the office, I found a brilliant story on the wire, with a Pellston dateline and under my by-line. I recognized only a few of my phrases in the story that made the front pages of most newspapers around the world.

From that point, through the twice-daily cycles that followed, it was Mahan's story, with his by-line. As it should have been from the first.

But, during those first twenty-four hours, I learned just about everything that was worth learning about wire-service journalism. About professionalism and humility, about a man who dedicated his life to becoming one of the nation's foremost experts on a crucial subject, and at the moment of truth, turning the glory over to a neophyte.

Pete Mahan never mentioned the sacrifice, never played the card of his clear superiority. Most likely, he never gave it a moment's thought.

I'm still in awe of Pete Mahan, and owe him a lot, including, probably, my assignment two years later to the AP's foreign desk in Rockefeller Center.

I've been thinking about Pete Mahan during the last week, and the ambition of young reporters, and others in similar boats, to earn their way to the big leagues, to make it to New York City, to the skyscrapers bolted so firmly to the ground and soaring so spectacularly, at times into the clouds.

Flying into La Guardia over Manhattan during my twenty-five years in the city, I'd always insist on a window seat ahead of the wing, just to catch a glimpse of "my building" that rose like a monolith from the streetscape below. I'd think of the irony: working securely at Rockefeller Center, polishing the copy of our correspondents, while they chased stories in life-threatening situations halfway around the globe.

And I reflected on the fact that, in their cynical turns of mind, the thing our foreign correspondents feared most was that the young guys slouched around the desk in concrete splendor would turn their sharp, careful reporting into glorified mush.

But, when they passed though the office on home leave, I sensed their envy of our ordered, secure life on 52nd Street and Fifth Avenue, or later, as a Reuters man, on 52nd and Broadway, or still later, on Water Street, a few blocks from the World Trade Tower.

The new playing fields for those plugging away in the

city, "adding value" to information from around the world, and those who collect it, are much more level.

The sanctuary of America has been breached for now and the foreseeable future. The dreams of many in the hinterlands to make it in Sinatra's city of song have been tarnished, if not turned into nightmares.

What would I be thinking if a bureau chief like Clem Brossier called me into his office today and said casually, as he did one day in 1972, "Well, my boy, they want you in New York City." Would my blood still surge with anticipation, with the thrill of knowing that I was being granted the wish of a lifetime? Or would I succumb to fears of sinister forces and choose to follow a different path, one of lesser challenges, one more secure in a known routine, in arguably safer surroundings and out of harm's way?

If I took up the challenge, would I live forever in dread, forced to watch every low-flying jetliner as it turned here and there, making sure it followed a standard flight path into a standard landing pattern?

I don't know what I would think, or for how long. Or whether geography makes a difference anymore.

All I know is that, at one time, I boarded a twin-engine cargo plane with only a passing thought of my mortality. Nature was the enemy then and I could see it, sense it, feel it. I knew the moment had a beginning and an end. But if there were a more insidious force lurking about so palpably, and for time without end, would I still go for the golden ring?

If my son or daughter were to ask me, "Dad, should I take the job they offered me in New York City?"—what would I answer? What would you say?

Are these the haunting thoughts of old age—or of a new one?

It's something that has to be on your mind, now and for a long time to come.

HALFWAY HOUSE TO HELL

Fortunately, for our sense of well-being,
appearances can be deceiving.

I HAVE PARTICULARLY LEARNED TO LOVE THE ECCENTRIC millionaires and brilliant thinkers who move among us, dressed in jeans or perhaps wearing the tweed jackets of absent-minded professors, stumbling through life utterly without pretense and inviting serious, if inconsequential, misjudgment. We may learn about their gifts only after they've left a bountiful bequest to a worthy foundation or someone finds an unpublished manuscript amongst their papers.

Something like that is happening in Mackinaw City, where a dilapidated wooden shack stands obscurely behind one of the numerous seasonal family-owned motels. It's now used as a shed for gardening tools; but a hundred years or so ago, it was the gateway to hell, a pesthouse, where people suffering from diphtheria or smallpox or any other contagious disease were sent. If they died, and many did, their bodies were quickly buried in the cemetery, conveniently located outside the pesthouse doors. If they recovered, they returned home.

The details of the pesthouse are unclear, but if Edgar Allan Poe had been around, he might have done justice to the harrowing accounts of those who spent their last days in hell to assure the survival of the community.

Ken Teysen, a village native who salts each monthly session of the Mackinaw Area Historical Society with fascinating tidbits of local lore, said he learned about the pesthouse in poring through eleven years of the *Mackinaw Journal of the 1890s*. There he found passing mention of someone being sent to the pesthouse, and on rare occasion, someone else returning from it.

"They went to the pesthouse to die," says Kurt Grebe, a retired physician who grew up in Mackinaw City and now heads the historical society. "They were simply taken out of circulation. It was the concept of isolating people to avoid exposing others to the disease that was the practice from the Civil War on."

Little is known about what care, if any, inhabitants of the pesthouse received, or the numbers who passed through it.

"A few brave souls attended to them with a minimum of exposure, slipping food to them in the door. When they died, there was not a lot of embalming done," Grebe said.

Teysen said that for years the local mortician would place a bid to the village council to attend the final needs of indigents for $25 a year. He told the council he had a reusable coffin with a hinged bottom that would allow a body to slide out into a hole.

Teysen said the term *pest* in *pesthouse* does not refer to crawly creatures but rather to pestilence, a virulent or fatal contagious disease and the name of one of the Four Horsemen of the Apocalypse.

The pesthouse was discontinued in the early 1900s, after the practice of quarantining people in their homes was adopted.

RYAN

H E IS A WORLD TRAVELER, ENGAGING EDUCATOR, graceful skier, unstoppable hiker, powerful essayist and photographer, and for ten months a year, a man absorbed in the affairs of the world, from high in the Rocky Mountains at the Vail Mountain School.

And, best of all, he's my son.

In the past few years Ryan, now thirty-two, has spent his summers in Southeast Asia, on the Indian subcontinent, and most recently in Turkey, where he hiked to the top of Mount Ararat, Noah's reputed landfall after the Great Flood.

"At 6 a.m.," Ryan wrote about his encounter with Mount Ararat, "the sun's warming rays hit us on the glacier, and they felt sublime. We were at 16,600 feet with one more peak of ice to climb. I was energized again, feeling more oxygen than ever. With one more step, I had made it!"

From the summit he crawled out on a rocky precipice and gazed at the plains that spread out before him several miles below. "For me, the mountains and volcanoes below looked like anthills that had sprayed their black ashes on Georgia, Armenia, Iran, and Turkey; four countries united by geography but divided by borders.

"Like in Nepal, I just sat in peace, thinking about life and the direction it would take me," he wrote, invoking an analogy from a previous trip.

Ryan persuaded his school to pay the airfare to summer destinations of his choosing, in return for lectures about his travels on his return. I was gifted with a copy of his 150-page journal that landed on my doorstep on Christmas Day.

In it Ryan made me his companion, alternating thoughtful meandering with witty asides, spiced with slightly naughty remarks about the women and men he met along the way.

During his travels, Ryan stayed in the youth hostels of what must be considered one of the world's true melting pots, where he met Turks, Kurds, Israelis, Palestinians, Iranians, French, Italians, Germans, Koreans, Japanese, Serbs, Slovenians, Croats, a few Americans and others. There, young people watched World Cup matches and expressed anti-U.S. views. Typical were the sentiments of a twenty-four-year-old Kurdish "Ice Maiden," a French teacher named Guzete: "Saddam Hussein is a very bad man for killing so many Kurds, but Bush is the same. He killed so many Iraqis with bombs. Saddam and Bush—the same."

Ryan found himself to be a fair match at backgammon against aging Turks, mesmerized by whirling dervishes, and captivated by tightly woven kilim rugs, two of which he purchased and tossed in his fifty-pound backpack to carry through the rest of the trip.

Ry had an insatiable appetite for kebaps (meat), rice and an occasional sewt (milk), which he said tasted "like it was a few months expired. I felt at home!"

Along the way, he wandered through dozens of medieval castles and ruins from the Hellenistic period. He even found a dust-covered, leather-bound book titled *How Darwin Has Plagued Society*, which held that Darwin led to the disasters of the twentieth century (communism, fascism, capitalism) by removing God from people's lives.

"The HUGE fallacy," Ryan noted after poring though it,

was that "the book failed to mention that religion too has resulted in war, social hierarchy, and mistreatment."

After 150 pages, Ryan distilled the lessons he learned through his fifty days of travel through Turkey and Greece. You might find a few of them worth reflecting on.

- We are all essentially the same. Instead of focusing on our minor differences, we need to focus on how we are alike and build more amiable relationships with one another.
- At the same time, diversity is a positive attribute that needs to be celebrated with open minds and not by firing guns.
- We should require a year of social service for our young people that will help us rebuild our reputation as a nation of positive influence around the world.
- We must learn that giving is more valuable than receiving.
- We must judge people for who they are, not by their government or stereotype.
- We must listen carefully to those around us, whether they be Israeli solders, Kurdish shepherds, Iranian refugees, or Turkish doctors.
- And we must never take our basic freedoms for granted.

Ryan tells a moving story behind each lesson. You will have to trust me that they all are convincing.

SUMMER'S END

WE WAITED OVER TWO WEEKS TO TEST THE WATERS. Nothing was as it had been, or was to have been. Swept along with the national agony, we imagined perils at every turn, so we delayed the inevitable sad parting at summer's end, to give us pause and time to reflect on our own fortunes. And on when we might see each other again.

The delay offered a small but real comfort: a brief reprieve, at a terrible price for so many, for an eighty-seven-year-old woman and her son, now pushing sixty. Yes, the president, our president, would have us move ahead with our lives—but did that mean we should take pleasure in the extra time we had together?

We did, though, despite misgivings. We postponed the weekend, as if that was the right thing to do, as if it could somehow calm our fears, however trivial they most certainly were.

We spent the additional days puzzling over early evening Scrabble, jesting with generations of family at the dinner table, wandering through the back roads of the Upper Peninsula, chatting with two grouse hunters who believed they had just seen a wolf at river's edge.

And, we gifted each other with memories. Dad's old raincoat from the back of the closet—and yes, it fit! My gosh! His name tag is sewn carefully inside the collar; a habit left over from Depression days.

And a dozen books, most of them outdated Northwoods histories, now surplus, squeezed from the modest bookshelf by newer biographies of presidents' wives and mothers. The older books were now mine, to read or to parcel out to friends and libraries.

In return, I offered Mom an eighteenth-century berry picker, freshly plucked from the Internet and said to be illegal in Michigan, to replace a hand-woven knick-knack on the wall. How daring!

We were somehow replacing the old with the new, and the new with the old, acknowledging the change in our lives with small mute tokens of deep significance.

But, Saturday did come, all too quickly. According to long tradition, I would drop my car at Pellston, drive with Mom in her car to Columbus, Ohio, and meet sister Cilla, flying in from Charlotte, North Carolina. Cilla would drive eight hours back to Charlotte in Mom's car, while Mom flew to Charlotte and I back to Pellston to pick up my car.

Something like that. Only the events of September 11 made even that routine seem to tempt fate. So, we reserved the right to change our minds, up to the moment that Mom was to board the plane on Sunday. If things didn't feel right, she and Cilla could drive home together.

As Mom and I settled into her car at Pellston, I suggested we try something new, a path never tested, a ride along the shore, east of Cheboygan, into uncharted waters, to Rogers City, Alpena, Tawas City, and all the lighthouses in between. It was something we had long wanted to do, for over seventy-five years in Mom's case, nearly sixty in mine. Somehow, the timing seemed right. Returning to the concrete, the brick and mortar, the noise, and the hurry of big city existence would be daunting for Mom. A leisurely drive along the shore of Lake Huron, through the occasionally turning trees and slow-moving small towns, might ease the transition.

And, it did.

BLUEBERRY PIE

THE SMALL CLUTCH OF FRIENDS WHO ATTENDED DAVE and Margy's holiday party in St. Louis left with broad blue smiles, the aftermath of gorging a parcel of Shirley's blueberry pies, air freighted in from Paradise.

Brother Dave proudly dubbed the toothsome grins "the St. Louis Blues" and attributed them to the fickle fruit of the low-lying shrubs surrounding the hamlet at Whitefish Point on Lake Superior.

Dave and Margy had their blueberry epiphany last summer at Shirley's Berry Patch bakery and chat room, where Shirley and her husband, Carl, turn out their lard-crusted delicacies through the night to meet the ever-growing demand for the Northern Michigan prized packages.

Guests at the St. Louis gala included the dean of Font-bonne College (Margy's boss) and other literary luminaries, all arriving in expectation that something wonderful was about to happen.

With Dave's glorious promotion of the event, I expect the St. Louis gathering looked high in the night sky, expecting to see the Magi shuffling to Earth with their camels, gifts, and victuals in tow, along a starry stairway leading from a brilliant nebula in the East.

Which is almost how it happened.

When I spoke to Dave the day before the event, he confided that he wasn't at all sure the pies would arrive fresh and in time for the celebration, and each in one piece. After all, last summer had been a no-berry season in Paradise, although Shirley confided that she still had several hundred quarts of the frozen blue nuggets left from the summer of '05—enough to bake pies until the new season is upon us.

But, unaccustomed to big city orders, Shirley felt considerable pressure to perform a near miracle for brother Dave, which she took as her challenge of the Christmas season. To ensure absolute freshness, for example, Shirley timed the baking and cooling of the pies to coincide with the arrival of UPS in the village, which was normally on a Wednesday and too late for a Tuesday delivery in St. Louis.

Shirley arranged for a special Monday pickup and prayed the van would arrive at four p.m.; not earlier, lest the driver haul aboard what would quickly become a bucketful of warm but delicious blue ooze.

Then, she left a message for Dave, who said later that he was delighted to hear Shirley's enthusiastic Yooper accent declaring victory over the shipping gremlins.

Shirley's husband spent the day creating pie cartons, designed to surround the pies firmly but tenderly to whisk them unsullied by aerial sleigh to the chimneyed house on Faculty Row at Washington University.

It all worked, and it has become a near-Santa story in a near-Santa village.

After the pies arrived safely in St. Louis, three of Dave's colleagues, including one who heard of the pies' arrival from a leak in the mailroom, dropped by for a sneak preview. Dave naturally filled his role as pre-party host!

"We each had a piece of Paradise and, before you knew it, half a pie was gone before the intended recipient, Margy, had even opened the container!" Dave wrote out of admirable shame.

At the party itself, a debate raged was over which was best: the pie crust or the blueberry filling. "Despite several rounds of sampling, the debate was not resolved and the need for an annual tasting was advocated by all," Dave recalled.

Margy saved one pie for their son, who flew in from Seattle, and daughter who drove over from Illinois.

Dave said the short-lived presence of the pie at the family gaming table made Margy's inevitable triumph at Scrabble the least painful of any such contest in the past twenty-five years.

The whole episode proved that a little taste of the U.P. goes a long, long way. At least 740 lip-smacking, heart-stopping miles on the fast track.

Mom

MOM'S RETURN

Quietly turning the backdoor key
Stepping outside, she is free . . .
from "She's Leaving Home" by The Beatles

A FTER YEARS IN EXILE IN THE NORTH CAROLINA DOLDRUMS, Mom is returning home, thrilled to be starting over again in Northern Michigan at the age of eighty-nine! I'm not sure if it was the cup of tiny blueberries that Ken Teysen, Mackinaw City's most gentle gentleman, brought back to her from an expedition to Paradise a couple of weeks ago that persuaded her to return.

Or the enthusiastic reception she received from her contemporaries and soon-to-be colleagues at Independence Village in Petoskey, after spending ten inspired minutes in full stride at the keyboard in the dining room.

Or the views of the creamy towers of the bridge jutting skyward from the constantly changing waters a stone's throw from her modest Wawatam Beach cottage, or Governor Jennifer Granholm's Labor Day signature scribbled on the crumpled piece of paper, wishing her the best.

Or even that glorious day at Pellston Regional Airport last month, where Mom posed for a picture with her grandchildren on the tarmac in front of the two visiting Warthog jets, and later likened the furnishings of the sparkling new terminal to those she remembered from the cottage her parents built in 1924 at Point Nipigon on the Straits.

Or, was it Ned Fenlon, the legislator turned jurist, saying a few kind words at his 100th birthday celebration at the college, making her (and dozens of other women) feel young again?

Perhaps it was inspirational vespers at Bay View, or the calming sermons at the Church on the Straits, or the afternoon visit to the elegant Castle Farms just south of Charlevoix.

Certainly, part of it was the rollicking family reunion in August, occasioned by the marriage of her granddaughter and attended by hundreds, including all four of her children.

I suspect it was all these things and more that lured Mom back to Northern Michigan from her big city North Carolina retirement village, where she was watched over by her loving daughter, Cilla, but found the intellectual doldrums almost too much to bear.

Mom attended Wheaton College in Massachusetts, where she learned to make thoughtful conversation about the events of the day and the popular books and music that flew off the shelves into the hands of young people. It was a skill she used in writing program notes for the Grand Rapids Symphony and the occasional book review she offered various groups through the years, and one that was under-appreciated in her North Carolina retirement home, where the daily staple in the small library was lusty romance novels.

On the way north in July, we stopped at the University of Michigan campus, where Mom visited the Martha Cook dormitory for the first time in over sixty-five years. The headmistress showed her the room where Mom resided during her final two years of undergraduate study, and invited Mom back this fall to perform at the rededication of the fabulous Steinway she played every night for the women who danced together following dinner.

In a sense, it's too bad no one is writing songs these days about the romance life offers to those past a certain age. But then, with all those wonderful tunes that were written in Mom's era to recall and embellish time and time again, I suppose it's not a loss but a blessing.

Everyone has the need to be appreciated for what they can offer, and Mom is no exception. She loves, for example, to prepare whitefish stuffed with corn bread as a special treat for guests, and waits expectantly for the praise that inevitably follows.

And she hopes to ship her baby grand player piano to her new home as the centerpiece in a living room I suspect will be a gathering place for residents who already anticipate her arrival. There they can drink in the sounds of the music of their era, as rendered by one of their own, as well as the classics produced by perforated paper rolling over burnished copper slots.

And all of this against a tableau of rolling hills and streets peppered with the Victorian homes outside her window.

Someone recently sent me an email from a far away place, commenting that he loved the Michigan North he had visited briefly because it "reminded him of family."

And that's the point about Mom's migration north.

A GRAND DAME

FORGIVE ME WHILE I DECOMPRESS. I HAVE JUST RETURNED from the Grand . . . For as long as I can remember, that pillared palace rested silently on the island in the Straits, so clearly visible on some days that one could almost count the columns and watch the flags flourish and furl; and yet, so blurred on others, one could only imagine it a furtive ghost playing hide-and-seek with the lusty foghorns.

Throughout my life, Grand Hotel was not so much an obsession as a curiosity—a mysterious jewel perched upon the giant turtle that lay nine miles off Point Nipigon, the summer resort a few miles east of Mackinaw City where my grandfather built Nanna a cottage in 1924 as an escape from hay fever that plagued Grand Rapids, their home town.

In eighty years of observing the island opposite the cottage porch, Mom considered Grand Hotel an exemplar of the unattainable, a place where the wealthy cavorted and, at one time it was rumored, lived well beyond the means and morality of mere Methodists such as we.

We made note of the Grand to our cottage guests, to be sure; but for the most part it was a figment, a mere condiment, even a sepulcher for the wicked, and best put out of mind. After all, Bay View was the chosen land for those of solid repute and unimpeachable intellect.

But on Monday, after all those years, Mom and I had the unique opportunity to set aside a lifetime of misconception and veiled envy to join the parade of the chosen few, and the luxury and hospitality that defines this American paradise. We paid a visit to the Grand.

There, in the company of travel writer Len Barnes and his elegant wife, Ellen; the prolific and brilliant writer Dixie Franklin, a protégé of Robert Traver (*Anatomy of a Murder*); the soft-spoken Bob Berg, once press secretary to Governor William Milliken; and a half dozen other accomplished professionals. I suspect I was selected as a geographical oddity.

We had been invited to witness the overnight awakening of the summer giant, a first for visiting scribes.

The Mussers, who have hosted five U.S. presidents and scores of notables in all fields of endeavor, treated Mom like a queen and the rest of us like dauphins. We were shown the attentive respect I am convinced all guests of the Grand enjoy from the Musser family and their marvelous crew.

My only moment of terror was the discovery that I had neglected to pack a tie, despite the legendary and entirely reasonable dress code that made ties de rigueur for evening wear. After a brisk walk through town in the rain I found that the summer supply of ties had not yet arrived. I politely turned down an offer by a considerate store owner to have a boatload of them brought over from his store in Mackinaw City on the noontime ferry.

Returning to the hotel, I pleaded my case to the desk clerk, who chuckled and advised me to simply borrow one from the service desk. There, an accommodating attendant offered me the choice of a black tie or one with colorful carriages woven into blue silk fabric, both brand-new and elegantly packaged.

Naturally, I chose the latter and, by way of compensation, I purchased something I could actually use—a history of what is now called "Grand Hotel." After all, I had worn ties for most of my life, if you include Sunday school, and chose to live in Northern Michigan to be free of the silly things.

Mom was a bit upset when she found there was but a single safety pin in her sewing kit (she needed two for some reason) and we tracked down a housemaid to rescue her. Can you imagine calling room service to ask for a safety pin? I couldn't; but I am sure that had we done so it would have been promptly and politely proffered. Mom was also concerned that she dress to the standard of the Mussers and their staff, including the Jamaicans, so smartly attired in crisp tuxedos and starched shirts.

Probably the highlight for Mom was the after-dinner performance of a young and beautiful harpist in the parlor off the dining room, bringing memories of her own mother who had been a concert harpist most of her life.

Mom was disappointed in not having the energy to find the Betty Ford Room, one of several decorated to the preferences of the First Ladies. It happened to be clear on the other side of the hotel.

We stumbled upon the Teddy Roosevelt Room, outfitted in the style of the sportsman-hunter, and the Hollywood Room, where the portraits of movie stars of Mom's era graced the walls.

When we inspected the Esther Williams Suite, Mom made a beeline for the bathroom to see if the famed swim star of the 1950s bathed in anything but a standard tub. She didn't. And somehow, Mom was pleased.

CASE OF THE MISSING CANE

But of all God's miracles large and small,
The most miraculous one of all
Is the one I thought could never be
from *Fiddler on the Roof*

OOMERS, BEWARE. BEYOND A CERTAIN AGE, YOUR WALKING cane, however so humble, will become an extension of yourself, a complete life-support system and constant companion, perhaps more valuable to your health than the dozen or so pills you will gulp as part of your morning ministrations.

Be warned: should that sturdy stick disappear without explanation you will find yourself in agony, despairing over its whereabouts and perhaps in the resulting confusion find yourself in mortal danger without an arm to lend support.

Mom, now ninety-three and determined to avoid using a walker, mollified her children years ago by adopting the black metal cane her father passed on to her as part of her legacy. She labeled it clearly with her name, address, and phone number in the event it strayed from her person.

As the past weekend came to a close at the family cottage in Mackinaw City, Mom called out to me, just before our departure, that her cane had gone missing. In trepidation I thrice circled the cottage, stopping in areas where Mom had insisted on raking leaves and twigs, an activity I had done my best to dissuade her from undertaking. I went through every room in the cottage, first searching corners and crannies, then making another round to undo beds, and finally to flash a light under anything the least suspicious.

Neither of us could recall the precise moment Mom had last been with her companion.

To calm our mutual obsession, I suggested she might have left the cane at the Berry Patch in Paradise, where I had made a huge racket the previous afternoon to bring Shirley, Michigan's Queen of Blueberry Pies, from the kitchen after she had locked the door against all comers. After all, I had retrieved Mom's eyeglasses from Shirley's restroom and thought perhaps Mom had left the cane there as well.

Unfortunately, the phone in the cottage had not yet been turned on for the season, and my cell phone was useless. I promised to call Shirley first thing the next morning.

I thought it unwise to admit to Mom that I had heard her shuffling through the cottage the previous night, with the telltale knocking of her cane against the wooden floor. As we drove off, I was certain the cane was somewhere in the cottage.

As we headed south on US 31, I suggested we stop at the airport and check out the restaurant, where we had had dinner with brother Bill and family on Friday. When I slowed for the airport entrance, I attempted to flick my brights, in minor road rage to chastise the driver who had just passed me in haste. But, instead, I activated the wipers, which sent a stream of water to the windshield.

And, as the wipers cleared the view, miracle of miracles, we saw the missing cane hanging precariously outside the extreme right corner of the windshield.

"Mom! Your cane!" I exclaimed, stopping the car abruptly. The cane fell to the road and I quickly retrieved it.

The episode left me with two possible explanations: either one of us had inadvertently laid the cane in the wiper well of the car, so that it was virtually hidden from view, or it had been returned from Heaven.

Even though the latter would represent a miracle just this side of the Virgin Birth, I preferred it as the most reasonable explanation.

Did I hear a fiddler?

THE PREMIERE

Moonlight and love songs, never out of date . . .
On that you can rely, no matter what the future brings
As time goes by.
from "As Time Goes By" by Herman Hupfeld

I T WASN'T SO MANY YEARS AGO WHEN MOM WOULD MEET guest artists upon their arrival in Grand Rapids, whisk them off to an early dinner in her modest white Plymouth, and then deliver them to Symphony Hall for their performances that night. It was a stimulating activity, and as author of program notes for the symphony for years, Mom gathered fascinating tidbits during her dinner conversations, few of which made print but many of them provided for lively exposition with her family.

Famed choreographer and dancer Edward Villella was her favorite, and she never tires of reminiscing about him, his wit, good looks, and charm.

That part of her life is but a pleasant memory, now that she has a budding career of her own as artiste extraordinaire of Independence Village in Petoskey.

Mom approached her premiere at the retirement home with studied trepidation, leaving her family and friends a bit nervous. "Will she or won't she?" we asked ourselves, hoping our insistence on the piano accompanying her to Michigan from Charlotte, North Carolina, in November would not have been in vain.

In fact, the polished top of her precious parlor grand had been deeply gouged en route and the near tragedy left Mom numb for weeks. After all, in her ninetieth year, she definitely does not appreciate surprises.

Mom found it ironic that her companion of more than half a century had withstood so many journeys without mishap, only to suffer an outrageous insult in what may have been its final move.

Mom purchased the piano during the Great Depression, from an aunt who couldn't play a note herself but switched on the electric player to entertain guests in European elegance with the etudes of Chopin and waltzes of Strauss.

Despite her studied trepidation, Mom enjoys sharing her gift with others and, on her arrival in Petoskey, we nourished her dream of returning to the stage with subtle words of encouragement. She could, we knew, quickly win over an audience of her peers with lively renditions of the popular songs of their era, most performed without music but all rendered with the natural gift of one born to the keyboard.

Although Mom would not be rushed into a performance, whispers spread from room to room, table to table, that Marion Lathrop was in their midst and would perform in due time.

During the days of waiting, I would peruse Mom's bookshelf, where I found thick tomes detailing the lives of U.S. presidents, a collection or two of opera libretti, and a single video—that of a legendary performance of Victor Borge, the accomplished Danish musician and comedian.

Mom's most vivid memory of a personal performance, perhaps inspired by Borge, was of the night not so long ago when the regular pianist at The Pier Restaurant in Harbor Springs fell ill and asked her to sit in for him, assuring her she was up to it.

She succumbed to the offer and earned $60 for the night, not counting the $2 tip stuffed into an adroitly positioned drinking glass from someone who requested a number not yet in her repertoire.

Lately, she practiced daily at an unobtrusive hour, so that if she were invited to perform, she could accept with confidence.

When brother Bill phoned that Mom's premiere was scheduled for the following day, I was elated. At 4:00 p.m. on January 5, an hour before dinner, I took a center seat in the communal dining room, surrounded by fifty residents who, for all their years and walkers and wheelchairs, were clearly in for a good time.

Mom warmed to the audience with a brief monologue and then plunged her long and graceful fingers into the keyboard, filling the room with the music of the thirties and forties. She dedicated the first song to her brother-in-law, my Uncle Howard, who had passed on earlier in the day, and then followed with such numbers as "Somewhere Over the Rainbow," "It Had to Be You," "Love Walked In," and "Sweet Georgia Brown."

The University of Michigan's Fight Song earned Mom enthusiastic applause from several alumni, two of whom were widows of deans of the university's School of Music, where Mom studied classical music while playing the piano for the young women at dinnertime at her residence, Martha Cook Hall.

"That was when girls danced with girls," she recalled. "It seems awfully funny now, but we had a good time."

She solicited requests on condition they not be songs from the last ten years, a condition easily accommodated.

For me, Mom's performance was a triumph of spirit over age and marked her true arrival in Petoskey.

Mom said the greatest compliment she received was a request from a waitress to give piano lessons to her boyfriend, who had been in the audience. "He wants to play just like you," she was told.

Wouldn't we all? I thought.

SUNDAY DRIVES

O VER THE PAST FOUR YEARS, OUR SUNDAY MORNING journeys from Petoskey to Mackinaw City for church have become a ritual. There are, however, unique aspects to the trips that raise them out of the ordinary, like my trusty, if rusty, 1994 Ford Explorer that's pushing 350,000 miles in its feisty middle age.

Promptly at 9:15 a.m., Mom, now well over ninety-three, emerges from her apartment to climb aboard my shiny blue beast. It's a bit tough for Mom to whip herself up into the saddle, but once ensconced, she is ready to revel in adventure.

Many years ago, Mom played stride piano for the Thursday night book club crowd, as well as for the Friday night fish fries, and other social events at the Church of the Straits. They still remember her, and she them; although like in the September Song, the days grow shorter.

We figure age has its privilege, and always park in the yellow-striped no-parking zone right outside the church entrance. Once inside, we shed our outer garments and find a spot in the last pew, which seems to be reserved for the chronically late, the shy, and the faint of heart.

There we sit through the service, now amplified for Mom and several dozen others sitting in the "enhanced audio zone." Never mind that the headset turns Pastor Dave into a male Lily Tomlin.

We sing Presbyterian hymns that as devout Methodists we have never heard before. After the service, we share a few precious moments with old friends. Some of those moments date back sixty years or more.

On our return trip, we stop at the Village Inn at Pellston Airport to meet my brother and his family for soup and a sandwich. If we are lucky, we can watch an airplane perform from the second-story window of the restaurant, where Mom has the Whitefish Chowder and I, the Indian Onion Soup.

Landmarks on the trip include the huge Levering chicken, which always brings a knowing laugh; and Dave Kling's Chevrolet dealership, where Mom notes the number of vehicles in the lot is the same as the previous week, and concludes sadly that Dave apparently hasn't been able to sell a single one.

Mom comments on the beauty of the unspoiled swampland north of Levering, and predicts that it will be subject to development over the next decade or so, and rejoices in the possibility she may not be around to see it happen.

She keeps a close eye on the speedometer. If the needle edges over 55 she'll ask me just what is the speed limit in these regions. I take the hint; but wonder why she can't wait for the car ahead of us to turn off the road to give us an unimpeded access to the roadway ahead.

"He's just doing the speed limit," I tell her. It happens several times a trip. I expect it reflects a Western sheriff's attitude to the righteous—or would that be the attitude of an outlaw?

VOTING

ELECTION DAY 2004 BEGAN AROUND 7:00 A.M., WITH A pleasant drive through Readmond's pine and birch forests to township hall, where four cheery women, each with a defined role, inducted me into the art of chadless voting. Optical scanning, they call it.

The wide open doors invited me and 447 other eligible voters into the elegant New England-like chapel that, wrapped in a glistening white clapboard robe, stood alone amid the wildflowers of Wormwood Lane as a surreal model of democracy.

It had been a successful trial run.

An hour later, I met Mom and drove her to the brick-and-glass Bear Creek Township Hall to perform her civic duty.

Mom sparkled in her stylish pink windbreaker worn over a light-green suit with a butterfly on the corner of the lapel. She considered spending a few minutes at the polls to be a sacred rite for which one must be dressed appropriately.

On entering the hall, we picked up a yellow sample ballot and went through the list of candidates and issues, going over the contested races to jog her memory.

Not that she needed it.

Mom had, after all, read every story published in the newspaper over the last few years and knew the particulars of the more dramatic contests and critical races. And the caution against splitting her vote between parties.

Election officials were cordial and correct, shooing me away when Mom sat down in the special booth reserved for the disabled and elderly. "You're not allowed to be with her when she votes," one said.

When Mom stood up a few minutes later, she inadvertently dropped her cane and inserted the prepared ballot upside down. When the machine, as programmed, spit it out, Mom became a bit flustered. An official scurried over, slid Mom's ballot back into its security blanket while pretending to look out the window, and advised her gently of the problem.

"Things are a bit different this year," Mom was assured.

It took a bit of doing to maintain secrecy, but Mom deftly removed the ballot from its folder, flipped it over, and tried again. This time, the machine gobbled the ballot without detecting an error. With Mom beaming in triumph, I was allowed to approach her and escort her to the car.

It was an episode virtually without pain, one that led Mom to remark on the sacred privilege every American enjoys as birthright.

A life-long Republican, Mom returned home to continue reading John Kerry's book about his experiences in and after Vietnam, a book that will undoubtedly figure in her determination of who is the right man to lead the country for the next four years.

I await her judgment with anticipation.

THANKSGIVING

BACK IN AUGUST OF 2003, EMMET COUNTY THREW A GALA evening cruise for everyone, big and small, young and old, heralded and unheralded, who had a connection with the dedication of the magnificent new terminal at Pellston Regional Airport. The guests included Petoskey's eminent hotelier Stafford Smith at one end of the scale, and Mom and her reporter son at the other.

Stafford smiled cordially during his quick introduction to Mom and me, and continued his roundabout, chatting with hundreds of folks aboard the Arnold Line ferry. He took no names during his excursion, and didn't need to.

Mom was duly impressed, having known the Perry Hotel since her first trip north to the Straits in the summer of 1923. (The hotel was established in 1899, only a few years earlier.)

Mom recalls the grief her family endured, compressed as they were in their black Buick, jump seats fully occupied, until they encountered the sharp curves of the gravel roads through Mancelona and Kalkaska. There, the kids had to dismount and push through the mud and ruts. Their next stop was at the Traverse City campgrounds, where half-canvas, half-wood structures for overnight travelers surrounded a communal dining hall.

Even more exciting, she recalls with glee, was the night

she and her sister Ruth, both under ten years of age at the time, bounced noisily on the Perry's aging innerspring mattresses. "We called it the 'Hotel of Squeaky Beds,'" Mom said she told Stafford on the ferry. "I asked him if he had changed the mattresses since then, and he assured me he had."

Three months after the cruise, Mom and I decided to celebrate Thanksgiving dinner at the Perry Hotel. Wonderfully festooned, the Perry greeted us with open arms as we were ushered into the Reycraft Room and seated at one of its well-appointed, linen-covered tables.

Mom, then ninety, took my arm as we strolled to the buffet, where Stafford, wearing the tallest and most highly pleated toque blanche this side of Versailles, was holding forth as chief turkey carver. Spotting Mom moving through the line, he exclaimed, "Well hello, Mrs. Lathrop. It's so good to see you again."

They say the number of pleats around a chef's hat signifies the number of ways a chef knows to cook an egg. In Stafford's case, I believe it signifies his proficiency at recalling the names and faces of people he has met, however briefly, in his career.

The unexpected greeting certainly made the holiday for Mom, and has been a tale often told in the family.

Mom, a celebrity, as she approaches her centennial!

In November 2006, Mom and I again had occasion to visit the Perry. We finagled the last available table, this time in the formal H.O. Rose Room overlooking the bay. But, as we inspected the sumptuous fare, we were disappointed not to find our now familiar face hovering over a slashing knife.

Nevertheless, as we approached the carving table, with dishes trembling in outstretched hands, a voice rang out with a familiar greeting: "Mrs. Lathrop. It's so nice to see you." And then, it added, "Stafford sends you his greetings—from Arizona."

It was general manager David Marvin who, wearing a slightly reduced toque blanche, explained that the Smiths were now spending their winters in Arizona; but they didn't want to be forgotten by their friends.

How he knew who Mom was, and had prepared a most suitable greeting, was beyond us; and it shall remain a secret of David and his partner.

But that secret will keep calling us back, year after year, for second and third helpings of turkey and the trimmings.

Relationships

MARY

"Could you take a friend canoeing, if you go?
Call me, okay?"
"Oh Lord! NOW you want to canoe!"
An exchange after months of cajoling.

FOR SEVERAL SUMMERS I CASUALLY WATCHED THEM BUILD our colossus. On clear days, you could see the caissons rise from the Straits, and out of their centers grew the stately, graceful towers. My vantage point was the white wicker swing that hung from the bead-board ceiling of the cottage porch at Nipigon, nine miles east of the construction site.

I had just turned teenager and our group of rapscallions paid scant attention to the historic feat, preferring instead penny-ante poker, Coca Cola, and rock-n-roll. But the occasional sightings were enough that I clearly remember them today. But the true enormity of the bridge came home to me two weeks ago, when a friend and I paddled the family's old red-canvas canoe, without planning on it, under the entire length of the bridge, from Fort Michilimackinac to St. Ignace and back.

"Well," my friend wrote, when we had settled on a date,

99

"Wednesday happens to be the Feast of All Souls, so we will be canoeing on a day that celebrates those who have died, and it was one who had died that told me in a dream that I had a lot of canoeing to do."

We exchanged emails as we watched the unfolding weather forecasts about our already unseasonably warm November, hoping it would hold for yet one more day. And so it did—high of 55, no wind, and mostly clear. It was perfect. I planned to pick her up at 10:00 a.m. and return her home by 3:00 p.m.

"Be sure to dress warm and bring an extra pair of socks!" I advised. "We will be wearing life preservers. And bring your Victrola and 78 rpm recording of Momma Cass singing 'Dream a Little Dream of Me.' I think it would be an absolute gas to hear her bellow 'Dream' to both sides of the Straits from our canoe while we paddle ellipses through the cool waters!"

As it turned out, the life preservers and gloves stayed at the bottom of the canoe and, with the rhythm of our rowing and the inspiration of the environment, we never felt the need for Momma Cass. My email to her the following day captured the magical adventure better than a narrative. From the long list of remembered snippets:

- Wet chilled toes
- Honest talk, wafted aft on a fickle breeze that carried with it the hollow thumping sounds of trucks passing over metal grids
- Green metal crosshatching that stitched elements of the underbelly together, and massive cement caissons encasing alabaster towers that soared like beacons to the sky
- The play of sunlight on ripples, that for my first mate evoked a delightful aphorism of her favorite poet
- Friendly shouts of truckers

- Crystal waters lapping the sides of our canoe under lazy skies and changing clouds as lonely freighters and silent islands drifted far away

- Our St. Ignace beachhead, with her toe print on it, and the race to the finish on the other side!

Oh, so many memories . . .

᷍   ᷍

For me, our spontaneous voyage under the Bridge was a rite of passage, and while my first thoughts regarding our journey are vivid, they are but an echo of what really happened.

It can be challenging to find experiences that carry us to the edge of the mysterious, the unknown, and the life threatening. And while in former and indigenous cultures survival through these types of experiences was a prerequisite for individuals that sought their place in community, in our own time we are hard-pressed to find this edge.

If I may be bold, our canoeing is an experience that will serve our personal lives in the future, the way unprecedented events in the hero's journey serve in fairy tales. The hero (or heroine) is, at last, beset with an impossible task before which he can do naught but fall to his knees and cry, when to his aid comes rushing all the prior virtue and courage he has exhibited, to carry him through the challenge victorious. In other words, to serve as his bridge.

The mighty columns of concrete and metal that plunge without peril into the deeps that threatened our wayward vessel awed me to silence, while yet I considered how free were we from the massive imposition of technology that so shapes and changes our days that we lose the relationship to straining muscle and sweating brow required of our forebears, the challenges that for them forged the foundations of community against the elemental forces of nature.

It was an absolutely glorious voyage and a rare gift. It's no wonder I waited so long from the time of my dream to actually go canoeing.

Thank you, friend.

Mary Stewart Adams

SIX DEGREES OF SEPARATION

O TTO, MY GREAT PALINDROME OF A FRIEND, HAS ARRIVED and departed. And as usual, after a day of reminiscence and refined contemplation, we concluded that all is well with our lives.

Otto comes to visit once a year from Santa Barbara, where he holds forth as a bartender in a "Friends" surround. I imagine him there as a kind of blithe spirit and professor/confessor.

This year, Otto outdid himself, leaving a trail of strange and wonderful encounters that even surpassed those of previous years.

He attended an early Thanksgiving party in Traverse City, where the twenty or so guests listed what they were thankful for. Otto, a native of Birmingham, Michigan, told them he was thankful to be back among people who so well represented Middle American values. It was an inspirational moment, and we all held hands and prayed.

The following day, we had lunch at Legs Inn in Cross Village, where Otto discussed the future of the world with my soothsayer friend from Harbor Springs. They agreed that humanity has a limited future unless true and historic human values can be restored. (My part in all this has been to abstain from television and other vulgarisms—recognized by my friends as a positive contribution and a statement of values but hardly one that qualifies me for a leadership role.)

En route home to California, Otto spent a week with his Santa Barbara friends in Vail, Colorado, attending a conference with spiritual leader and humanist Sai Maa. Always one to attend to his physical as well as spiritual health, Otto drove the streets of Vail looking for a gym to work out in. He couldn't find one, so he flagged down a driver to inquire. The driver turned out to be my son, Ryan, a teacher in Vail who recognized Otto from our visits to California during his youth. Ryan called me that night—for the first time in a year.

That chance encounter was only the latest of several that have reduced the "Six Degrees of Separation" to perhaps one or two. The one that raised hairs, where none have grown before, occurred when the subject of a long Weekender article for the paper asked where I had started as a reporter. When I told her Detroit, she asked where we had lived. I told her Grosse Pointe Woods.

She asked the street name, which I could not recall, but I told her the name of our landlady, a Mrs. Sleer, whose name I will never forget. "That was my mother," said my Northern Michigan neighbor. "And you lived in the house I grew up in."

At the annual fall Apple Festival in Charlevoix two weeks ago, my companion and I visited the Historical Society's booth, where she spoke with the group's president about the home she grew up in, located next to the casino in town that had a tunnel to her house used by Al Capone. She concluded her visit by purchasing a copy of a history of Charlevoix that included a picture of her former home and the casino.

While their talk ensued, I was charmed by a watercolor print of the U.S. Coast Guard Cutter *Acacia*, which has made Charlevoix its home for years. I noticed the artist's name, "S. Logie," and mentioned to the historian that I had attended the first day of kindergarten with a Shane Logie.

A stylishly dressed woman in sunglasses standing behind me said that she was Sue Logie, the artist, and that Shane Logie, her sister-in-law, was visiting her husband, the former mayor of Grand Rapids, John Logie, as we spoke. Sue promised to relay my good wishes to Shane after these many years.

And so, thanks to Otto-induced and other near encounters, the world appears to be closing in on me.

ANNA

And I can't be sure exactly,
but I swear I saw her say my name.
from the song "Stitched Up" by John Mayer and Herbie Hancock

M Y NEW FRIEND, LET'S CALL HER ANNA, LIVES AND breathes by the spoken word. A natural beauty, now flirting with middle age, Anna's been practicing the art of reading lips since she lost all but a smidgen of her hearing when she was in high school.

If you're at a party and Anna sees you say her name, she'll come over and engage you in a delightful conversation. So delightful, you would never know she is reading your lips. Once aware of the challenge, you form your words distinctly and quietly. That's all. Carry on naturally. Watch her eyes. They'll tell you when to repeat a phrase. Just remember: shouting doesn't help.

I am always struck by people who overcome their disabilities to lead near-normal lives. My quadriplegic brother, for one. Last seen in Paris, lecturing. As witty as he is profound. And Mom, pushing ninety-two, is another; reading history and giving tea parties for honored guests. And dropping a presidential name or two.

There are plenty of you who accept what has been given and move on.

Anna and I share an aversion to the disharmony one finds in large groups and gathering places. Anna delights in things that are especially endearing because they move within the sounds of silence. Like deer tracks in snow.

"I took a three-mile hike with my stepdaughter yesterday morning and then a three-mile showshoe at the state park. With all the deep heavy snow, it felt more like ten!" she wrote me.

"It was absolutely wondrous being in the woods with all the fresh snow hanging on the branches. We followed deer tracks for awhile and were finally able to catch a glimpse of him. My only regret was not taking a camera along."

I asked Anna, whom I've known only briefly, if she minded me sharing a few of her secrets. She said she'd be delighted.

After a small dinner party in Horton Bay, she wrote: "I have to be honest and tell you. I did not hear all of what you said. I usually understand bits and pieces and then try to put them together. Sometimes I get it right and sometimes not. It's like puzzle-solving all day. But, when conversation is fast or there are many people, I turn into the smile-and-nod mode."

If Anna missed anything, I'm sure I missed more. And what Anna gets, Anna retains. I can't claim the same.

When I bragged about my brother, she responded graciously: "I love to hear stories like your brother's. One of the most important gifts that I have been able to give is the gift of hope. I see a lot of infants who are being tested for hearing loss and it's very frightening for the parents. So, it's nice for them to see that you can still succeed in life in spite of the challenge."

I sent Anna a column I had written headlined "The 30 Percent Solution." It was about an observation by Mom's audiologist (and incidentally Anna's) that lip-reading is thirty percent of hearing.

"Thanks for sending the article. Unfortunately, for me, it's the eighty percent rule!" she said.

As a sensitive conversationalist, you can help Anna and others like her understand you better. Repetitions are made, after all, not only at the request of lip readers, but also to make a point that is worth making. As Count Basie said to his band at the end of the classic "April in Paris," "One more time."

ARE YOU MY FATHER?

O N ARRIVING HOME THE OTHER DAY, ANN, MY LANDLADY, met me at the door with the curious news that I had just missed a caller, Dan, who would only say he was here on personal business.

Dan told Ann he had missed me at work, asked about my living situation, and, after being told I lived upstairs, left his name and telephone number, and departed without leaving a card or a note.

Since his name meant nothing to me, I was concerned he might be someone wanting to even an old, even if imagined, score.

Ann suspected Dan was a bill collector. After all, few have paid me a visit at home in the four years I've been here.

As I had no unpaid bills and was concerned over the mystery of it all, I Googled his name and phone number and found someone of that description employed by a home construction company in Wisconsin. That made a certain amount of sense because I had recently looked at pre-built homes and figured he was touring the area intent on making a sale.

The next day Dan phoned me at work and said he had driven through the night to get back to Wisconsin in time for work. Curiously he said he was not the same Dan that worked for the pre-built home company. This was strange because he had an unusual last name and I was perplexed that two persons of the same name should live in the same state. An odd coincidence, perhaps, but certainly intriguing.

Dan told me he was looking for information on my high school classmates, particularly a certain girl, whom he identified. I recognized the name as someone from grade school, a budding artist who was best friends with the girl I later married.

"She is my mother," Dan said. "She gave me up for adoption at birth, something I learned several years ago. She adamantly refuses to disclose the name of my father, but she did say he was a classmate of hers."

Dan said he obtained a copy of our 1960 high school yearbook, leafed through the pictures of graduating seniors and stopped at my photo, which, he said, looked very much like him. After a pause, he said with polite assurance, "I think you are my Father."

I was dumbfounded. While there was no possibility that his hunch could be true, I sensed the keen anticipation Dan had at having reached the end of his long and painful quest. And, in that moment when he waited for my response, I wanted to reach out, give him a warm hug, and say, "At last! I've been searching for you, too!"

But, honesty prevailed and I assured Dan that I had never been romantically involved with his mother and, although his sleuthing was inspired, diligent, and admirable, it had yielded a red herring—me.

Despite the unsettling allegation, I found myself sympathetic to the man, twenty-two years my junior, and told him so. After all, it seems to me that everyone has the fundamental right, and in most cases privilege, to know his or her parents and enjoy the blessings of family.

I asked Dan, now happily married, gainfully employed,

and the father of two, to e-mail a photo of himself. I told him I would try to spot any obvious likeness to a former class-mate.

He agreed to do so; but it soon hit me that whether I could actually advise him of any such likeness was a highly complex ethical question that would involve serious soul-searching. Fortunately for me, Dan's photo did not spark instant recognition and, in fact, he appeared so different from me at any age that I could only surmise that his con-clusion was evidence of wishful thinking and desperation.

I sent a response that said, in part: "Hi, Dan. Thanks for the photos. I don't recognize anyone immediately that you look like. I've attached some photos of how I look these days. You'll see how fortunate you are to have a future all of your own! I was pretty much bald at your present age, and much heavier. I wish I could help, but at this point I'm draw-ing a blank. I do believe that every one of us has the right to know who are parents are/were. If you can think of any way I might be of assistance, let me know."

I have not heard from Dan since. I wish him Godspeed.

RUGBY

WHEN HE CREATED THE WORLD AND ALL THE BEASTS thereon, one of His greatest challenges—dare I say miscalculations?—was to give Man a lifespan many times that of his Best Friend. Over the following millennia, that single circumstance has brought the world to its collective knees every decade or so, as we mourn the loss of true friendship and despair at the futility of trying to renew it.

I remember when Rugby appeared to be practicing for that eventual moment, as he awaited my return from work at the end of our long Connecticut driveway. Rugby was a small white Lab who was convinced from birth that he was really a border collie. His mission in life was to forever corral our New England home. To Rugby, the white clapboard dwelling must have resembled a flock of sheep meandering through a field of green.

In the course of the day, Rugby would circle the house in blazing speed, stopping occasionally to survey threats from above and scold the army of squirrels he spotted taking refuge in the branches overhead. Rugby's mission was obsessive and required him to bark incessant alerts to perceived dangers, as the neighbors would be sure to tell you.

In any event, on that bittersweet day, I was fated to be alone with Rugby, who greeted me with panting anticipation as we walked along the shoulder-high rhododendrons at the edge of the driveway. With a nod of his head and a lively waggle of his posterior, Rugby beckoned me to follow him to the moss-encrusted brick patio that encircled an ancient oak. A sparkle in his eyes told me, "Come on, Dad! Quick! I have something truly exciting to show you!"

With his head cocked and a smile on his face, he plopped down on his haunches, a Marine at attention, several feet from a furry pile that had once been the object of his contempt. "I finally got one, Dad," he said, beaming with pride. I congratulated him, according him full regimental honors.

It was a moment of profound bonding between two living creatures of differing breeds, and one that would carry us through the challenges that accompany old age.

Rugby eventually developed diabetes, which required me to give him two shots of insulin a day under a fold of skin on his neck. Rugby never whimpered at the insults to his body, but only glanced up at me with trust born of our moment together on the patio.

His condition led him to dig a home for himself in the sand under the shed of our new Colorado home. It seemed to me he was aware of his condition and ashamed that he could not control his posterior, which he had to drag along wherever he went. From his burrow and with only his head in view, Rugby looked as good as new, the gleam in his eyes in anticipation of life's next challenge undiminished. But, he resisted any attempt to return to the family fold.

Finally, I concluded our moment had come, and asked my son Ryan to drive the three of us to the vet's. As we drove though the mountains, I held Rugby in my lap, and through the watery blur in my eyes I pondered the innocent, trusting, playful smile I had come to know so well. I remember telling Ryan, "Son, his front half wants to live forever, but his back half simply won't let him."

As father and son wept together, I remembered that day on the patio, when Rugby so proudly pointed to his lifetime achievement. I rubbed his neck and assured him, "Yes, Rugby, that was indeed your finest hour."

SEASONS

Springtime:
When memories fade and pretty dreams rise up.

OR SEVERAL SUMMERS IN THE EARLY 1980s IT BECAME A ritual. Our family of four would fly from Connecticut to California for three weeks of glorious vacation, enthused about the diversity of natural beauty and adventure that awaited us.

Along the way, from the Sierras to the southern coast, and Highway 1 to the north, we met many displaced Midwesterners exalting in their new surroundings and trying to entice us to join them. Although, in private moments, they would lament one enormous loss that was the price of relocation: the loss of the seasons.

They particularly yearned for the vibrant changing colors of autumn. In San Diego, the sun was the only season they knew, and from San Francisco north they endured a constant damp and misty chill, accented by a drizzling rain from November to March.

I thought about this the other day, when a friend recollected meeting Johnny Mathis after a concert some twenty or thirty years ago. We spent several hours discussing the haunting love songs we had once found so enchanting.

Hearing them again, I found the songs full of allusions to the changing seasons, often so subtle they had escaped me at a time when Mathis's lilting voice and extraordinary range and superb musicianship captivated me.

But now that words and ideas play such an important role in my life, I actually began to listen to every word and phrase and intonation and inflection, and in the process found an appreciation for the deep and beguiling insights, many invoking the elements of a Midwestern season, that Mathis breathed into his artistry.

"How can a Californian, or anyone limited to one or two seasons in a year," I asked myself, "grasp the depth of Sunny's despair over having lost her sweet lovin' man?"

"When Sunny gets blue," Mathis sings, "her eyes get gray and cloudy, and then the rain begins to fall." She "breathes a sigh of sadness, like the wind that stirs the trees and sets the leaves to swayin' like some violins are playin', weird and haunting melodies."

But having endured the winter, our Midwestern winter if you will, Mathis assures us that Sunny will be reborn, and that "her memories will fade and pretty dreams will rise up, where her other dreams fell through."

To those of us able to witness the annual rebirth of our green and luxurious countryside, through a long and changing spring season, we know deep down that Sunny's pretty dreams are rising up all around us, like the trilliums and crocuses and daffodils that are poking through the brown and brittle leaves of memories fallen through.

And, Mathis asks a new love, possibly our sunny summer, to "hurry here to kiss away each lonely tear, and hold her near when Sunny gets blue."

PERFECT RELATIONSHIPS

THE REACTION TO A RECENT COLUMN ABOUT MY RESEM-blance to Shrek, the popular green ogre of filmdom, was disheartening when a consensus developed that the likeness was accurate. But, there was also a curious interest in the phrase uttered by my friend—"We have now entered Phase Two of our relationship"—shared as an unrelated footnote to what I believed to be the primary revelation.

My intent here is not to challenge Ann Landers, but rather to provide guidance to others like me who are told they are entering, or have entered, the mysterious new land of phases. Is it like Middle Earth or is it somewhere between heaven and hell? were among the inquiries I received.

An eternally youthful ninety-two-year-old reader called as soon the column appeared, nervous because he was to meet his new girlfriend that night and he wanted to be prepared for the possibility that he, too, might be confronted with Phase Two. It bothered him, as it bothered me, that there should even *be* a Phase Two, as long as what must now be called Phase One was in good working order.

At the time I couldn't offer any guidance, except to speculate that it meant love's initial labors had been lost to, or at least diminished by, concessions to the inevitability of reality. I told him I would get in touch if and when I had successfully navigated the uncharted waters. And, I advised him to be prepared for the worst. We could both fall off the edge of the earth.

A few days later, a conceptual answer occurred to me as I was flying over the Mackinaw Bridge, landing on Mackinac Island and planning the next stop at Pointe Aux Pins airport on Bob-lo—all in my Flight Simulator 2002 Cessna 172, of course. The revelation was this: to perform as a virtual pilot you have to appreciate the dynamics of flight. They are really quite simple and, once understood, offer the near-perfect analogy to the factors governing the ups and downs of human relationships.

The best ideas are brief and clear, once revealed, like e=mc2, or energy equals mass times a constant squared, an Einstein theorem which those of you with higher understanding than mine will also find instructive. So, here's the heart of the analogy. Don't flinch. You probably read *Who Moved My Cheese?* This is much less painful.

The principal elements of flight are fourfold: thrust (or energy), lift, gravity, and drag— four competing forces that reach equilibrium in level flight, which I now understand to be Phase Two. I'll describe each principle briefly, so you get the gist:

Thrust: This is the most important element, the one the engine produces, the one you control with your joystick, throttle, enthusiasm, elan, appreciation for your partner.

Gravity: There is little you can do about it, short of crash dieting to lighten your load before takeoff.

Drag: You can do a lot about drag—life forces that work against thrust and forward movement. In an airplane, drag comes from the aircraft's resistance to air, and the faster you go, the more the drag there is. In human terms, drag is a combination of mortgages, kids, car payments, work situations, and the like—the real drags.

Lift: This is the component that results from the combination of the other three forces, so you'll need top performance from your energy sources at takeoff to lift you off the tarmac and fly you upward into the clouds.

So, control of the aircraft, as with relationships, comes down primarily to the energy created and how you control it. Subtle changes of attitude, both in the aeronautical and human sense, give you power to direct the flight—upwards, level, or down.

The flight instructor's advice to the novice is to always keep one eye on the "attitude indicator," the instrument that tells you which way you are headed relative to the horizon —up, down, or banking left or right. With the right attitude, a tank full of gas, relatively good weather, and a plane in sound mechanical condition, you can go anywhere the plane can fly. But, if you are distracted by small things, you'll lose sight of the attitude indicator and possibly control of the aircraft.

There are all sorts of subtleties that ring true, many expressed in understandable language. "Crabbing" should be avoided, except in strong crosswinds, for example.

And keep your chin up a bit—"nose up," to be aeronautical. Even in level flight, maintain a good attitude, keep those competing forces in equilibrium, and you'll fly right in every phase—on takeoff, in flight, or on a soft landing.

Attitude, equilibrium, and self-control are everything.

I once tried flying a Boeing 747 flight simulator for several hours at JFK in New York. Without understanding the principles of flight, I crashed in every city on the map.

So, it's worth a few hours in the simulator to prepare yourself for the real world of flight, and human relationships in all their phases. It's not too late. Just remember: the goal is not to fly solo but to do it in tandem. And all hands on the yoke, please.

Okay, Ann Landers. The stage is back to you.

Youth

ANTICS

Some Antics Are Best Left on the Cutting Room Floor

THE MOVIE *ANIMAL HOUSE*, FOR ALL ITS ADOLESCENT HUMOR, remains a favorite of mine for many reasons; but probably most because I believe I had earned a spot in the film. Chris Miller, my classmate at Dartmouth in the early 1960s, wrote the script based on his fraternity experiences, and I recognize a few of the mutual friends he immortalized in the classic parody of drunken toga parties and dissolute debauchery.

My friend George, for example, who often ran naked through the halls of my dorm in a stupor, once pursued a townie, spending time with her under the stars on the gridiron before he discovered she was thirteen. He ended up in the film. Chris claims that he himself was Pinto, but I knew it was George, just as many of you claim Pinto was modeled after a buddy down the hall.

My pranks, which I thought highly original at the time and later considered natural for the film, never made it as far as the cutting room floor. But, because they have been a well-kept secret for over forty years, I thought you might like to know.

They begin with Scott, my roommate, who, true to his

name, was a penny-pinching lad of Scottish blood, very studious and scorning irreverence of any kind.

For my part, I pinched pennies, not because of any genetic proclivity, but because my allowance was minimal and working as a dishwasher in the dining hall hardly helped fund any excess.

So, we pooled our proclivities and circumstance, and came up with plans to save a considerable sum of money by forgoing the extravagance of our pre-paid meal tickets. The first inspiration came to me when we took a table near the end of the conveyer belt that carried half-empty trays along the perimeter of the cafeteria into the kitchen for processing. I noticed that every twentieth tray or so carried an untouched meal into the maw of oblivion, the interior of the kitchen where each plateful of unwanted and often untouched food was scraped into large pails destined for the pigsty.

I invited Scott to join me in discreetly helping ourselves to the untouched meals and, when we assured ourselves the plan was viable, we slipped into the dining hall without having our dinner cards punched, anticipating a large dividend at the end of the term for meals unclaimed.

It worked for a while, until the mistress of the hall got wind of our scheme and kept a wary eye out for us. She ushered us out on more than one occasion, but we managed to elude her most of the time by posting friends up the line who could warn us of her presence.

The hugely successful operation, the buzz of the campus, came to a screeching stop when Tiny, a 300-pounder of gigantic appetite, plagiarized our idea and one-upped us by sitting at the next table up the conveyer belt and wolfing down whatever appealed to him. Which was just about anything.

He was delighted at his coup—his smirk was unavoidable—and we were left furious and famished. But, there was nothing to be done, as Tiny always used his meal ticket to gain entry and we were hardly in a position to rat on him for his excesses.

So, we adopted Plan B, which was simply to eke out our sustenance from a large plastic cooler that we placed between our desks while our unused dining coupons accumulated. Once a week we would fill the larder with staples from the local grocery, warming edibles on a hot plate when necessary. The plan committed us to long stretches of fasting; but to celebrate a successful week of diminished diet, we'd steam lobsters in a tin can when the local purveyor drove by on a Friday.

That too worked for a while, until our friends learned about the treasure chest and paid us visits, ostensibly to discuss esoteric subjects but, in fact, to subtly lift the top of the cooler and withdraw an apple, pear, or banana while pretending they had no idea they were stealing our next meal.

Then came midterm exams. Under the pressure of studies, we sealed the cooler—at the time it was full of eggs and bacon and a rapidly melting block of ice—and returned to the college dining hall, using our tickets for our daily fare.

Our good friend Ray, however, was unaware that the free lunch in our room was no longer on offer. And so it was, on a warm sultry day, that I approached Middle Mass, the classic red brick and green-shuttered dormitory where Scott and I shared a fourth-floor room, only to be met at the door with a smell so putrid it could only have survived in the Alpha Delta house. The odor increased in virulence as I ascended the stairs and, in dread of the truth, I turned the corner at the top of the stairwell to find the doors to our room and the bathroom inside wide open.

There I discovered the shower in full stream, targeted at the cooler. Its top was hanging to one side, exposing a green mold-like substance that frothed up from the cooler and the shower drain like the slime in *Ghostbusters*.

Ray had paid visit, and finding us not at home, had nonetheless dipped into the former honey pot, only to find the ultimate weapon of mass destruction inside—a rasher of putrefied bacon. The thought of Ray racing to the bathroom with the cooler in tow, blindly twisting the knob of the shower, setting the cooler beneath it, and running pell-mell from the dorm still delights me.

But, as others in the dorm joined him outside, with hands to their faces, hoping for a breath of fresh air, I sealed the cooler and quietly headed for the cemetery that lay behind the dorm. Not finding a fresh grave in which to bury the evidence, it occurred to me that I had actually been blessed with a weapon of retribution for every slight I had ever endured at the hands of preppies and posturing pedants.

Like an agent of the devil, I prowled the campus, peeling off one strip of putrefied bacon at a time, hiding them in the most unlikely places in the empty rooms of my adversaries—the innersprings of their mattresses or the interior of their guitars.

When I went to collect my reward, the anticipated awe of those struck by the most hideous odor imaginable, I found no satisfaction. All the victims appeared to have taken an oath of ignorance of the scourge that had mysteriously descended on them.

Several weeks later, as I was riding on the glee club bus, one of the intended victims took a seat next to me and told me about the incredible odor that had inexplicably overwhelmed one of his friends in a room down the hall. As he recounted the story, I pretended fascination but privately realized I had misdirected my retribution and wrapped the evil bacon around the innersprings of an innocent.

You don't know how lucky you are; but I'll get it right for Chris's prequel, I thought.

FIRST FLIGHT

T HE TINY BRONZE WINGS, PINNED TO MY JACKET BY A shapely stewardess, were a gift from Capital Airlines. They marked nothing spectacular for the world, only a certain rite of passage for a young man who would treasure them forever.

I remember the small black-and-white photo of me with a goofy grin, standing outside the silver-skinned, two-engine tail-dragger of an aircraft that became a symbol of fantasy flight for me. So cherished are the events of that warm summer day, that I now spend hours in a DC-3 on my Flight Simulator, flying home to Grand Rapids, north to Marquette, or over the Caucuses in Central Asia. And, so obsessive has this plane become for me that I have a two-year-old, half-finished model of a DC-3 at home, its balsa ribs covered with onion-skin paper topped with layers upon layers of clear airplane dope.

It was the summer of 1954 when I made my first flight— ever. At the age of twelve, I gamely boarded a Capital Airlines DC-3 in Grand Rapids, Michigan, and flew north to Pellston, where Nanna waited to whisk me to her cottage at Point Nipigon on the Straits near Cheboygan.

Since then, I've flown in DC-3s and prop planes of any variety whenever I could, envying the adventurers of yesteryear whose spirits led them to fly to exotic destinations.

Even now, I can close my eyes and recall that first flight, when sitting in the first row, the window curtain drawn aside, I could take in the glorious view of the pilot and engineer in the cockpit, and the stunning stewardess who gave me my "wings." Out the window, the left engine coughed and wheezed and belched a cloud of oily smoke as it cranked to life.

So, you can imagine my thrill when Charlie Stratton showed up last week at Pellston Regional Airport, to offer his late father's Capital Airlines uniform to airport manager Kelley Atkins, for display in the terminal building. When I asked Charlie whether it was possible that his father had flown me on my first flight, the one from Grand Rapids to Pellston, Charlie said it was entirely possible he had picked me up on an unscheduled stop in Grand Rapids, even though he flew regularly from Willow Run to Pellston.

What made the possibility even better in my mind was that his father, Joel Buck Stratton, Capital's youngest captain, married the woman of my teenage dreams, the stewardess who stood at the top of the folding stairway to welcome me aboard.

One thing that isn't fantasy: Back in 1954, and for years afterward, it cost only $20.19 to fly one-way to Pellston from Detroit aboard a DC-3. That included the ten percent federal tax, a sandwich, and on a clear day, a view of the Straits.

Even accounting for inflation, it was a hell of a deal.

ROAD CREW

PICK ANY SUMMER MORNING FORTY OR SO YEARS AGO, AND you'd find me bouncing around in the back of a black pickup truck with four or five other college guys, all bronzed and muscled, heading out from the Kent County Road Commission garage for an honest day's work spreading pea gravel with large scooped shovels on fresh-laid tar.

It was going to be an honest day's work alongside the cornfields of rural western Michigan. Honest, that is, if WE had nothing to say about it.

While fanning gravel in graceful patterns from the back of the truck, we'd check the skies, note any promising cloud formations, and pray for rain. It was a daily ritual, a bit silly to be sure, but we got so we could predict a drizzle or squall within ten minutes of its arrival.

And when it came, we'd look at Paul, our taciturn foreman, and watch as he'd squint at the sky, grimace and nod, and then, with a hint of disgust, squeeze out a spray of tobacco juice through his tightly pursed lips.

It was a sign that we had beaten him again.

We'd hop inside the cab, pull out bologna sandwiches from our lunchboxes, and munch away while we leafed through the pile of tattered girlie magazines, remarking on some interesting aspect of displayed anatomy and laughing at raunchy jokes till the sun came out again.

"Tall Paul" would tap on the glass that separated the ruling class from the peons in back, and we'd climb up on the mounds of gravel in the raised boxes of the waiting dump trucks.

Paul rarely spoke. He communicated through facial expression and sign language. It was an animal act and we were his happy seals, observant and obedient, thankful for the occasional scraps he'd toss our way—like five minutes out of the sun.

Those few precious moments dressed the salad days of my youth—Dad's greatest gift to his firstborn son was a lesson in the value of a dollar earned by blood, sweat, and occasional respite.

As I piece it together today, it was an obvious setup. Dad knew a road commissioner and his wife—he probably delivered their babies—and through him the word was out: Doc Gray's son could use a job.

It was all camouflaged, of course. I was led to think I got the job thanks to my good looks, brains, and initiative. But clearly, the fix was in.

GARDENS

*Warmed by the spring sunshine he sat in the carriage
looking at the new grass, the first leaves on the
birches, and the first puffs of white spring clouds
floating across the clear blue sky.*
Leo Tolstoy, describing Prince Andrew in *War and Peace*

THE SIMPLE YET ELEGANT WORDS OF TOLSTOY TRANSPORT me back to spring awakenings from the dreariness of long-ago winters. White spring clouds float in memory across the clear blue skies of the Granite State, over the lush Alpine meadows of Bavaria, and above gnarled scrawny pines of the parched Colorado Rockies.

Yet, the sky most frequented in my memory is the one above Dad's bountiful garden, a half-lot fantasy inspired by his east Tennessee childhood home that he carried north with his medical degree to adorn our family's otherwise respectable suburban home in southwestern Michigan.

That sandy patch was home to virtually every vegetable and fruit that grew from seed, and yes, to thousands of creepy-crawlies. It was surrounded by peach trees and plum trees and overrun at times by grape arbors and a hundred mail-order chickens. It was a miniature Chekovian "Cherry

Orchard," if you will, complete with anxious aunts and philosophizing uncles and focusing on the tensions of changing times, as the 1950s were—at least on our half-acre.

By profession, Dad was meticulous, scrubbing his hands and under his nails often and with great care. He indulged himself by trusting the cultivation and harvesting of his southern-farm fantasy to his wife and children.

That wasn't easy for Mom, whose family tree grew from *cultivated* soil, the roots nurtured by music and literature and fine Grand Rapids furniture.

In a perverse fashion, I took great joy when the chicks escaped from their basement cages and flew from ground-level windows to the yards close by, all with a huge racket that summoned the normally placid neighbors to their fences to inquire about the barnyard animals littering their carefully kept gardens.

It was natural that Mom was mortified by the whirling clouds of feathers that occasionally issued from beneath our home. And it was natural too that she called upon her children, of whom I was firstborn and the "most responsible," to recapture the truants and return them safely to their nests alongside the basement furnace.

Brother Dave remembers how he was "chosen" to do all the weeding, because sister Cilla was a girl, Bill was "just a baby" and I, your humble author, was "incompetent to figure out a plant from a weed!"

"We all know you had figured out how to get out of planting, weeding, and watering—you stuck to eating and did a damned good job of that," Dave says, in a pathetic example of total memory collapse, inspired by continuing sibling rivalry.

But, there are a few things we both recall in tandem. "Remember the black oozing fungus that grew on the corn?," he asks. I do. "I wondered how we could eat corn after seeing that. And the look on Dad's face when he found the perfect tomato? Or how he would tap the melons and try to get us to figure out what a good-sounding one was. I never could hear the difference.

"The best part of the garden was the taste of the 'REAL food' as Dad called his (really our) produce. I remember many years after we moved, Dad saying in early Yogi Berra talk, that 'food these days doesn't taste like food.'

"You know, he was right," Dave wrote me. "When was the last time you tasted anything as good as freshly sliced tomato and cucumber salad? How about Mom's peach jam or, even better, her peach pie? Or hot corn with real butter dripping down as you swirl the cob around looking for the last bit?"

It is with these memories that I joined the Blackbird Farm of Petoskey, one of many community supported agriculture ventures in the state.

I can't wait to hone my weeding skills.

SOUNDS OF NEAR SILENCE

LUCILLE PRANG INSTILLED IN ME A PROFOUND RESPECT FOR absolute silence. And in the process, she taught me the fine art of whispering, which I've used as a survival technique to subvert the threat of absolute silence and promote sanity in an increasingly tumultuous world.

Miss Prang, or the "Prang-o-Tang" as we referred to her well out of earshot, was the librarian at East High School and, as such, the peacetime equivalent of Ilse Koch, the notorious wife of the commandant of Buchenwald.

Eagle-eyed, matronly, and forever clad in royal-blue and pearls, Miss Prang was an imposing master of all she surveyed. She ruled with such terror she once caused an errant classmate to piddle in her place.

Hers was a world in which sound implodes: if nature abhors a vacuum, as Spinoza would have you believe, Miss Prang celebrated it.

The sounds of silence in her library were awesome: the turning of a page; a muffled cough; a sniffle; a stolen whisper; and, most importantly, the buzz at the end of the period that signaled the lifting of prison gates.

If ever a case could be made for child abuse, Lucille Prang would have made it, with convincing pride and supreme confidence. She also would have won a Nobel Prize for inventing the so-called "peace process," long before Oslo, although Miss Prang might have defined it differently.

Yet, the Prang-o-Tang must be given her due. She taught respect for silence and reverence for the unspoken word— something TV sitcoms have corrupted and made impossible in today's libraries and other public institutions.

She seemed to believe that a student staring at an open book in the silence of her library was proof enough that knowledge was being transfered, just as you and I assume that a bowed head in church is a sure sign of prayer in progress.

With the sounding of the buzzer, the dam would burst and a flood of speech-starved students spilled from the library into the corridors, refreshed and bubbling with pent-up conversation and laughter.

Following library, we were occasionally fortunate to find the congenitally oblivious Mr. Fairman substituting for "senorita," our Spanish teacher. He, too, suffered the sounds of silence; but unlike Miss Prang, his was brought on by the natural aging process unrelieved by hearing aids.

We called him "The Owl," in part for his sleek grey hair and the bushy eyebrows that jumped up and down over large-pupiled eyes that prompted a quizzical response to any stimulus. What made his nickname especially delicious though was his wont to move in quarter-circle hops that coincided with the movements of his eyebrows as he tried to ferret out the source of strange forest sounds in the classroom.

With a bit of skill, anyone with the incipient flair of a puppeteer could learn to manipulate Mr. Fairman to hilarious effect. There was a coterie of students spotted strategically about the classroom who could create owl sounds by softly crooning "to-whit" or "to-who" into cupped hands, their fingers artfully splayed to control volume.

The effect was magical, with owl calls and answers always made behind Mr. Fairman's back, unseen by the victim but, with our skill at volume control, never unheard.

A "to-whit" voiced from one side of the room would cause Mr. Fairman's eyebrows to flap as he hopped in short arcs to locate the source of the call. As soon as The Owl completed his turn, he found his students, including the perpetrator, fully engrossed in study. Then, precisely timed, a fellow hooter across the room would answer the call with an exquisitely voiced "to-WHOOOO."

Mr. Fairman spent what we considered the better parts of the hour hopping to our stereophonic calls, seemingly never certain whether he was hearing things or had fallen victim to a class of no-good-niks.

That was forty-five years ago, in simpler, quieter times. My, how things have changed! (Even my dear mother, who considered Elvis and the Beatles to be apostates in their time, now enjoys and performs their music to groups of like-minded retirees.)

So, let's turn down the volume on our children's boom-boxes for a moment of silence to honor the Prang-o-Tang and to relieve The Owl, wherever they may be.

WEATHER REPORT

The fragile ivory crust of winter will be rendered but muddy swill today by torrential rains . . .

THAT WAS THE WAY THIS FLEDGLING WIRE SERVICE REPORTER rendered an overnight weather report in the spring of 1970, much to the bemusement of the Associated Press membership in Michigan. The item escaped the immediate notice of Detroit Bureau Chief Clem Brossier, who devoted his attention to more weighty matters. In fact, I think it is fair to say that Clem hadn't read one of his bureau's weather reports in years.

He trusted his staff.

But a few days later, Clem beckoned me to his office and, peering up at me over his reading glasses, pulled a letter from a file on the desk. My weather report had been torn, apparently in haste, from the AP printer at the *Benton Harbor News-Palladium* and was clipped to a memo addressed to Clem. On it was a single oversized question mark.

"Is this yours?" Clem asked matter-of-factly, his face expressionless but for a telltale eyebrow that moved to the top of his forehead, where it competed for amply available hair space.

Expecting some kind of literary award for having turned

a mundane weather report into elegant prose, I responded that it was indeed mine. After all, I thought, my aristocratic Russian professor, Dmitri von Mohrenschildt, had opined that my essay on Leo Tolstoy was so good he thought it was plagiarized. But, because he didn't have time to prove it, he gave me an A and let it go at that.

Until the weather report in question, I thought the essay was the best thing I had ever written and, even today, consider the suggestion of plagiarism by the late tsar's tennis partner to be the finest compliment ever paid me.

So, although you may laugh, in that moment with Clem Brossier, I felt that I alone had smashed the fetters of a century of precise but boring newswriting with a single weather report, and I was exaltedly awaiting my just desserts.

Swept with pride, I felt instant solidarity with Karl Marx, who more than a century earlier had exhorted the world's workers, among them reporters and editors, to unite, for "you have nothing to lose but your chains."

Fortunately for history, Clem didn't see it my way, and he brusquely waved me away, grumping almost absentmindedly, "Well, never again." As I slinked out of his office, I saw him move quickly to more serious business in his day's file.

The episode reminded me of an earlier humiliation when, having spent too much time fathoming the lessons of the law, I penned a playful love poem and forwarded it to Ginny, a casual acquaintance with literary aspirations who had been temporarily committed to an asylum for the mentally insane.

The poem, little more than a simple "good night, sleep tight," went like this:

> *Dry my martini, darling*
> *While I set the sun.*
> *Then we'll lie in bed*
> *And blow out the moon.*

Ginny was allowed to telephone me a while later and we chatted as friends, catching up with what we could say about our lives. Near the end of the conversation, Ginny confided that she had passed my poem to her psychiatrist for his evaluation. He concluded, Ginny whispered with malicious glee, that: "You are crazy."

After these experiences, I vowed to go straight—and succeeded to the point that a colleague on the AP World Desk once asked me: "Do you always use trite and obvious words and phrases?"

All this leads me to today, when I had a compulsive urge to reflect, in this space, on the insidious effect of corporate fraud on our faith in public and private institutions. I was tempted to borrow the lead to my thirty-two-year-old weather report, which struck me as the perfect metaphor for the greed and deceit that creates the muddy swill in which our markets wallow.

But, then I saw the specter of Clem's raised eyebrow, and heard Ginny's whispered reproach, and recalled Dmitri's suspicions—and I thought better of it. Personal history had taught me a few lessons about mistakes I rather not repeat and, besides, I'm too old to again challenge the accepted rules of the writer's craft.

I'll have to settle for "dragonflies as big as hummingbirds."

Still, I ask myself: Where have they gone—those fragile ivory crusts of winter? We all weep for what was, and could have been.

SURVIVAL

There is real value in being lost at sea—to you if you survive, to the sharks if you do not.

IT WOULD PROBABLY BE CLASSIFIED AS CHILD ABUSE TODAY, BUT back in the 1950s, the rugged counselors at Camp Manitou-lin, located on a small lake somewhere in southwestern Michigan, firmly believed in initiating fourteen-year-olds to the values of self-reliance.

Promising that if I survived I would attain the pinnacle of success—the rank of Sachem celebrated at an end-of-season campfire—my Zuni Indian counselor blindfolded me and drove along a twisted course to a remote two-track an hour or more from camp.

There, he removed the blindfold and dumped me off in a field of tall grass, instructing me not to ask questions of anyone but to find my way back to camp using only my wits and a compass. I had two days to succeed.

As I remember it, I carried nothing but a canteen of water and a few Saltines. And, there was not a stranger along the way to offer me a hint of where in the world I might be. I was on my own.

I made it back to camp, although I have no idea how. All

I remember is the intense mid-August heat, stifling humidity, thick pollen that provoked endless sneezing, and the cool shade of a spreading yew under which I spent hours in a semi-conscious blur summoning my courage.

I also recall how delightful it was to return to my lumpy cot and later feast on a Sloppy Joe, bowl of Jell-O, and a cool glass of milk.

I think this early Outward Bound program worked. I reveled in my return to the civilized world of campfires and institutional food and, perversely, the pleasure of isolation and individual challenge and success.

The next chapter in self-realization found me facing a tweedy Ivy League physics professor who spent most of his classroom hours leaning nonchalantly against a raised black marble slab, peering over his spectacles at the steeply cascading tiers of preppy sophomores.

It was to our immense conceit that Professor Sears had written the textbook used around the world, with tough end-of-chapter questions and answers tucked away in the back.

To truly be lost at sea in New Hampshire was to spend hours navigating the professor's questions and not finding safe harbor. The answers in the back of the book were meant to be the terra firma, your reward for solving the problems. Instinct honed by learning helped plot my course, as I tacked this way and that with an eye on the polestar.

And, with a little luck, I navigated to the archipelago of answers. Except once.

There was one time I just could not find the Promised Land. Try as I might, my answer to a problem did not agree with Professor Sears'. My classmates were no help: I believe they worked backwards from the answers to the questions.

Somehow I mustered the courage to confront the good professor in his office after class and admit my exasperation.

He took my book, scanned the question, and flipped to the answer. He puzzled for a moment, then reached behind him and pulled out his wallet, removed a dollar bill and offered it to me.

"I always reward a student who can prove me wrong," I remember him saying as he escorted me from the room.

I had proved the Great Man mistaken with a question— and that was the lasting lesson I took away from college physics: the power of a simple question can be as effective as a well-structured argument.

The Sachemhood of Camp Manitou-lin failed to compare to the exhilaration I experienced at that moment of triumph, which even today I mark as one of the highlights of my life.

The next edition of the legendary textbook contained all the right answers, and no one but Professor Sears and I knew why.

The Mackinac Bridge looms through the morning mist in June.

Grand Hotel invited Fred and Mom to spend two luxurious days and nights to witness the sleeping giant awaken from its winter slumber. *(See "A Grand Dame," p. 80)*

The family's 1937 Old Town canoe evokes many memories. *(See "Mary," p. 99)*

Fred and friend Susan Manturuk enjoyed an "Anatomy of a Murder" weekend of their own making at the Thunder Bay Inn in Big Bay north of Marquette, Michigan. *(See "Impulse," p. 211)*

The July Fourth flag-raising ceremony at the Historic Village in Mackinaw City.

Double-crested cormorants flock to the White Shoal Lighthouse in Lake Michigan, located twenty miles west of the Mackinac Bridge.

Fred's siblings Dave and Cilla have a private discussion in Wawatam, the 125-year-old beach association west of Mackinaw City.

(l to r): Fred's grandson, Bo; daughter, Tallie; son, Ryan; Fred; and sister, Cilla, vacationing on Mackinac Island in July 2008.

Top left: Mom arrives at Pellston Regional Airport for her homecoming to Michigan on Friday, October 31, 2003.

Top right: Mom

Bottom: Mom's piano premiere at Petoskey's Independence Village in 2004.

Fred's brother Dr. William Gray and family make bi-annual medical mission trips to Haiti. *(l to r):* William, Madame Dorlius, Carol, Luke, Junior Dorlius, Zach, and Katie.

Dave

Fred

Shirley Clark, who with her husband, Carl, owns and operates Michigan's finest pie bakery, The Berry Patch, which is located in Paradise, near Whitefish Point on Lake Superior. *(See "Blueberry Pie," p. 72)*

On the Straits of Mackinac beach, Fred's grandson, Bo, collected crawdads, mussels, and oversized clamshells; and even saw Canada geese fly with the moon on their wings. These were a few of "Bo's favorite things."

Fred and Shrek. *(See "Is There Life After Shrek?," p. 189)*

Fred's son, Ryan, in Nepal. *(See "Email From Southeast Asia," p. 18 and "Ryan," p. 66)*

A Gray family portrait.

Ken Teysen investigating a toolshed that a century earlier had been a "pesthouse" or "pestilence house" for the incurable ill. Totally refurbished, it is now the centerpiece of Mackinaw City's Historic Village. *(See "Halfway House to Hell," p. 64)*

Bill Eppridge and his photo of The Beatles.

HUCKLEBERRIES

I F MEMORY SERVES, THE CURTAIN ON MY LIFE LIFTED WHEN I was four years old, picking wild huckleberries with Mom on a blistering August afternoon alongside the twin bands of steel that carried the daily freight trains between Michigan's upper and lower peninsulas. It was just after the last Great War and Dad had finally returned from attending to our wounded in France and to German prisoners of war on troopships in the Atlantic.

As Mom tells it, the three of us—younger brother Dave, Mom, and I—spent the war years shuttling between shabby apartments in Battle Creek, Kalamazoo, and Grand Rapids and, during those blessed days in summer, at Nanna and Grandpa's cottage at Point Nipigon on the Straits of Mackinaw.

In the pantheon of my aging memory, looms a haunting "elephant's eye" window above the screened front porch, staring sleepily at the constantly changing waters before us. There was a stone fireplace spacious enough for a pig on a spit and, at one end of the porch, a wide wicker swing was fastened by chains to a lacquered bead-board ceiling.

That swing became our ore carrier, which we manned at either end and, by pushing and pulling the chains, caused it to move rhythmically through the imagined waves and into the haze beyond.

But the moments that linger longest and most lucidly in my memory are those spent picking huckleberries amidst the sand burrs along the tracks and filling the white enameled canister that swung freely on a wire handle.

In the hush of the early day, I could feel the approach of the morning train in the emanations set up by minute vibrations carried along the rails. As I remember, I would touch the tracks to confirm with my other senses that the great moment was at hand and then step back in anticipation.

Soon the rushing hulk of metal would round the bend and surge toward us, belching clouds of steam, clacking over the rails as it swept past—and then quickly departing, leaving us in silence and in a child's awe of having encountered something profound.

Five decades later, although the forest setting has barely changed, there are no rails, no trains, little silence, and few huckleberries to be found in our patch or elsewhere in the northland.

So it was I drove with a friend over the Mackinac Bridge to the Wild Blueberry Festival in Paradise, near Whitefish Point, to try to recapture those first memories. There I sought advice from the locals who made and sold jam or pie or syrup, on where to find the elusive fruit. I knew they would not easily yield their secrets to a total stranger but I was unprepared for the artful obfuscation the questioning inspired.

"You'll find them everywhere," said a woman from Munising.

"The season's about over," said a man with a frown.

"The season has barely begun," chirped another.

"They love the sun," one woman assured me.

"They love the shade," her husband said.

Then, in unison, they gushed, "They love BOTH the sun and the shade."

"You'll find them behind the state park," said a woman, proudly cutting a pie.

"I last found some in the cemetery," whispered one kindly lady, who intuition told me was telling the truth.

One should always yield to the inner self when dousing for water or hunting for wild huckleberries, and something told me the obscure cemetery was the way to go.

I was right. Off a two-track road, miles from Paradise, among pine-shaded tombstones, were hundreds of blueberry bushes just popping with ripened fruit. I sprawled out before an abundant patch, picking the berries, one by one, and transferring them from the palm of my hand to a plastic bag that had replaced the enameled tin. If one or two fell into my mouth, it didn't matter. For I had found the profound silence, the quiet of those early years, amid the blueberries of Paradise. Enough to evoke those first moments of life.

Only the train had been left behind.

REMARKABLE MEN

WHEN I WAS A YOUNG MAN, DAD SAID TO ME, "SON, YOU can be anything you want to be." Dad was a man of few words; he taught by example. From Tennessee farm boy to big-town obstetrician, from the Depression that took the family farm to the relative wealth of East Grand Rapids, Dad lived the American Dream and served his community with confidence and skill.

Women loved him, men respected him. He packed a lifetime of joy in a brief sixty-three years.

When Dad passed along his advice to me, I knew he was thinking in terms of doctor, or perhaps lawyer or engineer. But I often wonder what he would have said if I had told him I would have settled for emulating Al Kaline or Eric Severeid. They were my heroes. They were the men I wanted to be, and they both had one thing in common—ultimate grace: Kaline, for his unspoken eloquence on and off the baseball field, and Severeid, for his eloquence in articulating the meaning of momentous events.

You had to watch Kaline and listen to Severeid to appreciate what extraordinary men could do. Baseball never held the fascination for me after Kaline; television news faded with the passing of Severeid.

Pity.

And then, a few weeks ago, East Jordan's own act of grace, Chip Hansen, returned from Lakeland, Florida, with a treasure that restored the glow. Chip had attended a Tiger fantasy baseball camp and rubbed shoulders with our mutual hero, the man who set the standard for baseball, the man who fifty years after winning the American League batting champion at age twenty-one, the youngest player history, still carried himself as a champion.

Immeasurably more valuable than the baseball inscribed with Kaline's autograph, a treasure indeed, was Chip's testament that my childhood hero was alive and unchanged. Chip professed that Kaline remains a man of grace, revered by teammates and fans as one of the sports world's ultimate heroes. And the least outspoken.

Chip said there was no other word to describe Al Kaline. To say that a person has grace is to bestow the highest possible tribute.

Grace carries a mystery, by the best definition the "unmerited divine assistance given humans for their regeneration or sanctification, a virtue coming from God."

Grace is a gift.

Few men or women have it. But it is something you know when you're struck by it.

I recognized Kaline's greatness while firmly holding down last place on the bench of the freshman high school baseball team. I was spared permanence in the position for a brief moment when our coach put me in right field for the final inning. Our team was leading by so many runs I was sacrificed to spare further embarrassment for visitors.

Not a lot happened in right field that day, but one of the last batters lofted a ball high into the sun, and it would be my only shot at playing my childhood hero.

Friends tell me they had seldom seen anything more amusing, as I circled right field, tripping and stumbling, as

I searched for a speck in the sun, my glove held high in prayer that the ball would somehow find its way home to the leather.

I don't remember whether it did or not; it didn't matter.

I realized that I had just met Al Kaline, and that I was no Al Kaline.

Later, when I stumbled into the news business, I often realized I had met Eric Severeid, and that I was no Eric Severeid. (That's a longer story.)

Those were meetings with remarkable men—and the chance encounters with standards of excellence and grace left impressions that would last a lifetime.

THE BEATLES

THEY SAID THEY WANTED TO HOLD MY HAND, AND I GLADLY let them. More than Elvis or even Little Richard did in the '50s, the Beatles led me through the musical landscape of the '60s and into the new millennium.

I was living in Munich during the winter of '64, working as a copyboy at Radio Liberty. I shared a fifth-floor walkup apartment on Agnesstrasse with two other North American innocents, in a Bohemian sort of way. The single room had everything we needed, except privacy—which we really didn't need or want.

Skip George, from Sudbury, Ontario, was there, a Chaplinesque character who was very funny when inebriated—which was most of the time. And there was Don Johnson, a lanky Californian, hanging loose, as most of them do.

My Russian language instructor, who had been a translator during World War II, lived on the floor below. He suffered my ineptitude with good humor. I think he needed the money.

A burly German ex-prisoner of war would barge in occasionally and ask us to spy on his former wife, a gorgeous language teacher, all for lessons he paid for.

The girlfriends would come and go. They said they were into films. We were never quite sure, and it didn't matter.

Outside the great door of our building, to the left, was a walk-down bierstube, where we hung out, sipped sweet German beer, talked endlessly, and listened to music. It was in that tacky, smoke-filled room, savoring rich beef goulash-suppe, that I first heard those immortal words ring out in the darkness, like a banshee wail: I sensed that the world, my world at least, had suddenly changed. For a long moment I sat paralyzed by an electrical buzz that surged up and down my spine.

I spent the rest of the night plunking pfennigs into the jukebox, trying to grasp and absorb their genius, the incredible combination of brash audacity and musical invention that was to transport a generation to a new consciousness.

When those four lads from Liverpool teased us with a low-pitched unison aside, "I think you'll understand," then burst out with "I want to hold your hand" at the top of their lungs, breaking into that ringing chord at the end of a seemingly mundane phrase—it was a single climactic musical moment that shook the world.

Little did we know they were proposing not to a teenaged nymphet, but to everyone.

Thereafter, the Beatles became a monument around which all popular music was measured, and usually found wanting, as their lyrics and melodies became increasingly sophisticated, without losing their originality, spontaneity, and charm.

The trail that began for me in the Munich bierstube led me through the pleasure spots of an age, with side trips to circuses and strawberry fields, in yellow submarines and on diamond-encrusted clouds, as we explored the lonely and profane, the cosmic and the karmic. It was a remarkable journey, led by remarkable men, and one I hope you enjoyed as much as I did.

Politics

"GET BACK TO WHERE
YOU ONCE BELONGED!"*

WHEN THE FRENCH RECENTLY CHALLENGED THE UNITED States at the U.N. Security Council over the possibility of war with Iraq, they failed to realize they would also be taking on Northern Michigan.

The potential for real damage to French historical interests lies here in the neglected north, and is a much greater threat to the overweening French than the comparatively puerile idea being circulated in fashionable circles of turning French fries into American fries. As my colleague Thomas L. Friedman of the *New York Times* opined in a column recently: "It is legitimate for Europeans to oppose such a war, but not simply by sticking a thumb in our eye and their heads in the sand."

Although Tom had other advice on how to remove the thumb, those who would rather effect long-lasting change than gain a headline or two from ephemeral protests in black need to consider the half-realized but devastatingly potent threat to French pride of Anglicizing such names as Charlevoix, Mackinac and Les Cheneaux.

Those names go back hundreds of years and represent the continuing toehold of the French in North America. With names like Gros Cap and Epoufette and Seul Choix and

*A column under this title inspired a front-page banner with Fred wearing a tam, smoking a cigarette, and trying his best to look like a disgusted Frenchman.

151

DeTour, the southern shore of the U.P. alone is replete with villages and historical markers that seem better suited for the coast of Normandy.

Many names that began as French were dealt with long ago by the common man unschooled in the intricacies of a foreign tongue. No one with roots in the North would dare try to pronounce *Bois Blanc*, when they have the commonly accepted *Bob-lo* immediately at hand. A mapmaker's correction is long overdue.

And why would any of us struggle with *Les Cheneaux* when *The Snows* will so nicely do?

From the national security standpoint, the lovely Seul Choix lighthouse near Manistique is clearly better rendered as *Sish-WA* by native Yoopers than from schoolbook French. Try to find Sish-WA without a map, *mon ami*! Don't ask.

Those of us who live proudly below the bridge have our Anglophilian ancestors to thank for exchanging the final "c" in Mackinac for a "w". Those who live north of the Bridge should consider adopting the proper spelling, not only in the spirit of the anti-French protest of today but for the sake of longterm linguistic uniformity. United we stand, after all. Eh?

Yes, here is the ideal opportunity to strike a blow, not only for our national pride but also for the clarity of our precious American language. While we have become accustomed to double-decker billboards touting one thing Mackinac on top and another thing Mackinaw on the bottom, pity the poor Frenchman and tourist of lesser origin who can't fathom the difference and wouldn't believe that both are spelled correctly even if pronounced the same.

If the French, who bridle at such words as *weekend* and *le hamburger* in their own domain, were to invade our sanctuary with fistfuls of erasers and white-out, we know where they would base their operations, don't we? Yoopers take note.

Not that the rest of us are immune from the confusion spawned by lingering French influence.

152

I remember a National Public Radio talk show host from Wisconsin making sport of the power failure that befell Mackin-ACK Island two summers ago. After all, he had been there once. To be generous, he may have been lodging his own anti-French protest by pronouncing the name as written. But I doubt it.

The most obvious plum for pickling is the hugely French name of *Charlevoix* (the Beautiful), named after Pierre Francois-Xavier de Charlevoix, who sought a water route to the Pacific nearly two hundred years after Columbus failed. The very thought of Anglicizing the name of our fair city, lake, and county will likely infuriate local patriots, but given the immensity of the French challenge to our president and our national honor, do the substitute names *Charles View* (the Lovely)" and *Lake Charles* really sound so bad?

I guarantee a common convulsive tic by the French when they read the headline in *Le Monde*, "New World Abandons Mother Tongue" (roughly translated from what the French consider the mother tongue).

After all, there is precedent, one which may be instructive to our erstwhile German ally, now marching in lockstep with the French: Goetzville, the tiny town north of Cedarville, was initially pronounced *Gets-ville* after the Goetz family which settled there in the late 1800s. But according to historian Thatcher Goetz, the pronunciation was changed to *Gatesville* during the period of anti-German sentiment during World War I and remains so to this day. Except for *Goetz*, which Thatcher pronounces *gets*.

So, I'm willing to do my part should it come to exercising our right to purify the language of the North. I pledge that if we are each called upon to make an historic sacrifice, I will ask my mother's family to change the spelling of their name from *Bertsch* to *Birch*. And should that prove unsuccessful, I shall give up Boeuf Burguignon for Lent.

SHAMELESS ADS

EVERY TIME RUSH LIMBAUGH SUSPENDS HIS ENGAGING commentary to give much too much time to the Excellence in Broadcasting Network's shameless profit center, I picture him glancing at his comb-over visage reflected in the golden EIB microphone and pondering the question posed at least hourly on his airway: "Is your hair thinning? Then why haven't you tried Avacor?"

It is one of the few questions to which Rush has yet to respond.

And then I think of Dr. Dean Edell, "America's Doctor," who has been dispensing good advice on the same talk radio network for years, telling his listeners of the fraud inflicted on all of us by purveyors of patent pills and snake oil.

"Aren't they listening?" I ask myself in incredulity at how gullible much of Rush's seemingly sophisticated audience must be.

"Are you hounded by creditors?" is the refrain of the financial consultants who have learned the secrets of the low interest payment plans that credit card companies don't want you to know—but can be yours for a price.

"Welcome to the Cortislim lifestyle. You meet those successful Cortislim users everywhere," goes an ad for a $50 bottle of fantasy pills. Funny, I've never met one. But I'll wager that most of the price one pays for the pills goes to Rush and his cohorts living in style.

It is stimulating conversation surrounded by moronic messages, such as the guy who rants with Michael Savage about the millions the federal government will give away if you want to write a book or start a hair salon. Just ask him— for a fee.

There is something wrong when Savage lavishes praise on America's soldiers for fighting and dying for Iraqi liberty, and then advises Americans to invest in gold in order to profit from these perilous times.

The talk show audiences obviously don't judge their hosts by the companies they keep, or should we say, keep them. There's a disconcerting disconnect between talk show hosts, their audiences, and the commercial messages that surround them—and it's worthy of a Ph.D. dissertation.

If we wanted to imagine the kinds of people these radio pundits attract, we could get a pretty good idea from the incessant commercial appeals to the corpulent, the dead-beats, the follically challenged, and the sexually dysfunctional.

That's quite a zoo.

These poor souls spend their days listening to talk radio when they could, and should, be investing their time in things truly profitable—starting with an honest day's work. Or at least a few hours of exercise, or tidying up their play pens.

"Three hours a day, every day, that's all I ask," Sean Hannity, the self-styled Great American, implores the addicted. "Now, more than ever."

"Now, less than never," I respond.

PREDICTIVE POLLING

I THINK OUR DEMOCRACY WOULD BE BETTER SERVED IF POLL-sters found something other to do with their lives than choke us with a steady stream of unreliable predictions of electoral outcomes.

Not that all pollsters should be stood up against the wall. Just those who compete with astrologers in predicting the future, and whose main function seems to be to supply the newspaper and broadcast media with pretentious headline fodder.

The other kind, the pollsters who provide data for reflective analysis of what has happened, are probably worth keeping around, assuming they are close to the mark, because they deal in trends and explanations, not divination or "clever conjecture."

The truth is, predictive pollsters are seldom close, and often far from the mark, in forecasting the final outcome of major races. This is not a cheap shot inspired by vagaries of election night reporting, although few but pollster John Zogby had much to crow about. Zogby was the one who on election eve detected a slight edge for Al Gore, when three other major polling organizations predicted a Bush victory by a significant margin. (The little devils were at work early on in the campaign.)

Beginning in August of this year, almost every day I arrived at my news desk to find a fax from the "workhorse," Senator Spence Abraham, detailing the latest poll purporting to show him ahead of his opponent, Democrat Debbie Stabenow, by a margin of between 8 and 15 percent.

We don't write stories about polls, and that in itself is refreshing for you as well as me, so I set these hot flashes in a wire basket reserved for post-election review of how the candidates conducted themselves.

On Wednesday, the day after the election, I had accumulated a six-inch pile from Spence, much of which detailed the polls he likely relied on, inspiring confidence in an easy victory. To be sure, Stabenow had a pile as well, claiming she was about to catch the workhorse, and her numbers proved to be equally unreal.

My favorite example, which makes my point well, was an unscientifically conducted poll and it had a laughable margin of error. Four days before the election, the Abraham Senate 2000 committee sent a faxed press release headlined "Abraham Wins! Michigan Students Reelect Senator Abraham in Statewide Election. Mock Election Winner Always Wins Real Election"

Some 50,000 Michigan students participated in the "mock election," it said. And the margins? Abraham 60 percent, Stabenow 40; Bush 52 percent, Gore 41.

The release concluded, in prose mindful of Soviet agiprop specialists: "Students are really reflecting their parents' opinions about the candidates, and that's why it's a good precursor of Election Day results. It's also a terrific activity for young people because it engages them in the electoral process and teaches them about the political system."

Well, how wrong can you be? What does it really teach our students, and the rest of us, about the electoral process?

"So what?" you might ask. "It's harmless. They provide us with some entertaining diversion."

"Well, exactly," I respond. The essence of democracy is that all citizens have the right to examine candidates and issues, and register their preferences through the ballot, unswayed by diversionary factors. Who knows how much this kind of posing influences the ultimate outcome?

I say, "Out, damned spot!"

I am aware mine is a Utopian view of democracy, one that if adhered to would gut an industry devoted to churning and spinning, and in the end, demeaning the electoral process with misinformation.

All I can say to these pollsters is, "Spin and churn. Churn and spin. And shred your credibility. We've got your number, even if you don't."

But, I'm afraid it will happen again and again. The evil genie is out of the bottle. The bat is out of the box.

There's gotta be a better way.

BREAD TAX

Mr. McGuire: "I just want to say one word to you . . . just one word."
Benjamin: "Yes, sir."
McGuire: "Are you listening?"
Benjamin: "Yes, sir. I am."
McGuire: "Plastics."
Benjamin's father (later): "Don't you think that idea is a little half-baked?"
Benjamin: "Oh no, Dad. It's completely baked."

from the 1967 movie *The Graduate*

NOW THAT CIGARETTES ARE GIVING MORE OF THEIR PROPER due to state coffers, it's time we recognize there's another dangerous substance that's been given a free ride for far too long, and it should be called upon to stand by tobacco against the wall of sacrifice for the well-being of the citizens of this state, and for the health of the state budget.

Are you listening, Jennifer? It's called "white bread." Once it was considered the staff of life. And, like tobacco, white bread has been proven to be the opposite of its original value.

Now that all has been revealed by the granolas of our world, we recognize that white bread is an unhealthy habit, if not addiction, and a primary cause of the obesity that is strangling the people of Michigan, making us the fattest state in the nation. According to the Associated Press, scientists say white bread and other refined grains seem to go to the gut and hang out as belly fat.

Governor Jennifer Granholm, who acknowledges that obesity is one of the top three health problems facing the state, has laid much of the burden of balancing the state budget on smokers, reasoning that the additional costs of healthcare are directly related to the use of tobacco.

Fair enough.

But, while many of us in the older generation wax nostalgic at the thought of a PB & J sandwich traditionally served between thick slabs of glutinous white bread accompanied by a frosty glass of whole milk, today we should, in my view, modify that craving, or if we cannot, we should pay through the nose when succumbing to it.

Consider this: we are a state of ten million people, and although I can find no reliable estimates of the number of loaves of white bread consumed weekly in our state, for the sake of argument, let's say it averages about one loaf per person a week. Why, that's over 500 million loaves of white bread a year!

Now, if we were to tax each loaf by only fifty cents, or about a quarter of its retail price and of the $2 we tax a pack of cigarettes, we'd come up with $250 million—a nice start towards balancing the estimated $1 billion deficit Michigan faces in the next fiscal year.

I'm sure you can think of other fat-engendering products—Big Macs, Whoppers, and pizza come immediately to mind—which would be candidates for a big "fat tax" that could slice the state deficit to the bone.

The idea of linking health to taxes has already been sanctioned by our lawmakers, and it takes only the slightest leap of imagination to see the potential it holds for solving all our fiscal and health-related problems.

For those of you crying "Foul!" there is a second part to my proposal that would introduce the element of fairness to thin people, who should not be penalized for the excesses of us fatties. I propose we institute an Obesity Quotient (OC) that would be embedded into the plastic strip available for data on our driver's license. Anyone with an OQ of only 40 (out of 100) would be let off scot-free of tax at the checkout counter; but a white bread eater with an OQ of say 80 would pay the full tax.

The OQ could be updated quarterly, for a fee payable to the secretary of state, to bring successful dieters into the tax-free zone.

The beauty of the scheme is that government need only calculate how much of a deficit the state faces, and adjust the OQ, the list of evil substances, and the levels of taxation on each accordingly.

Who of us fatties would object to paying an extra quarter for a Whopper in a fit of desperation? Or conversely, who among us would not entertain the thought of ordering a no-fat salad instead of the Whopper if it promised to lead to an appealing figure at a reduced cost?

Would the fast-food franchises care? Not a fig. Salads produce as much profit as burgers, I'm sure. And bakers can simply produce more seven-grain loaves for newly enlightened consumers, and for those about to be.

After all, why should Californians be the leaders in health consciousness?

Given my scheme, we Michiganders could set a standard of personal elegance for the world, if only we tightened our belts under the guidance of the benevolent taxman.

BILLBOARDS

WHEN YOU'RE QUIETLY DRIVING ALONG THE HIGHWAY, do you see what I see? Of course you do. Does it make you see red? I hope so.

All I think about when I see billboards is how much they obscure and cheapen the lovely countryside. About how they affect our quality of life. And of the arrogance of any organization that would assume its message is worth polluting our natural surroundings for a visual airing of some internal bickering.

"Out damned spots!" I say. "Give us back the beauty of our natural heritage."

Billboards have become dinosaurs of the Burma Shave era. We should put them out of their misery—and ours.

Let's quickly dispense with First Amendment arguments. Does our right of free expression allow anyone to cry "Fire!" in a theater, or to post a message on any byway, in any way, however offensive and distracting and minimally informative it may be to the community at large?

I don't think so, and neither do most municipalities which strictly restrict signage to accommodate local sensitivities. We are not breaking new ground here. Many communities, in their good sense, limit signs to the business and property of the landowner.

Somehow, though, the billboard crowd is afforded greater rights to pollute once outside the city limits—yet it's precisely the views of the countryside that are the ones most worth preserving.

I am frequently overwhelmed by the plethora of billboards that impart very little information, but undo the well-intentioned efforts of planning and zoning boards to preserve our natural heritage. What does it matter if a developer is limited by height and width and setback and green belt restrictions, if the approach to the development is plastered with billboards announcing thirty miles in advance that St. Ignace is located across the bridge? Or that a McDonald's is only twenty-nine miles away?

Let's face it: by now there's a McDonald's in every town in the country. If you've forgotten the fact, most highways have logo signs at exits to jerk your memory. There's no need to remind us of an obvious truth with a huge and unsightly billboard.

And what of a billboard that recommends you call a phone number if you are having trouble with your marriage?

The basic tenet of billboard advertising, and advertising in general, is founded on building the old knee-jerk "recognition factor." It doesn't matter much what the content of a message is, as long as the name of the business sticks in your brain, to pop into your consciousness when you get a primal urge. Well, for me, all that repetition sticks, not in my brain, but in my craw.

I wonder if advertisers ever consider the possibility that billboard advertising can generate "negative recognition factors"—reactions to billboards so patently offensive that the offended would never patronize the businesses being advertised.

It's akin to abuse of the Internet highway. If you broadcast an unsolicited ad or commentary to the world, you subject yourself to the ultimate punishment: a full-scale "flame"—a blizzard of angry responses that will choke your system and encourage you to use good manners in the future.

I for one will never submit to a primal urge for a Big Mac, solely because of the visual pollution the ubiquitous eatery subjects us to. Let McDonald's or Burger King or Big Boy buy as many radio and TV commercials, and magazine and newspaper ads, as they can afford. We can avoid them with the flip of a switch or the turn of a page—but we can't avoid those Golden Arches or the cute little fat boy in the middle of otherwise beautiful farm or forest land.

Perhaps we should outlaw billboards, and buy up the rights to those that already exist and then destroy them, under the principle of eminent domain, defined as "the right of a government to take private property for public use by virtue of the superior dominion of the sovereign power of all lands within its jurisdiction."

What is a better public use than being able to view the countryside, our most precious natural resource, unimpaired as we drive along our public ways?

Or what if we were to set up some kind of rating system, as exists for movies, that would calculate the size of the billboard, times the relevance of information imparted, times the proximity of the sign to the service being advertised, and rid ourselves of those with a sub-minimal rating?

How many would be left?

Only the small, tasteful, and informative state and county road signs that let you know where you are, or that you can eat, sleep, and drink just off the next exit at the franchise of your choice.

What would be left? Everything you actually want to see. As the sign says, "Hold your money." And call your legislator. That's freedom of expression.

⌒

NINA

Ⅰ N THE GRUELING SUMMER OF 1963, NINA TAUGHT ME A LOT about American values. There were six of us, American college students who had been cleared by an American intelligence agency to spend a month touring the Soviet Union in a shiny red VW bus, one of the first allowed in the country.

Always accompanied by the "thoroughly reliable" Intourist guide Nina Tsap, we did the usual tourist sights— Moscow, Leningrad, and Kiev—and managed to do some unusual things as well.

Each of us spoke Russian, some better than others, and we drew crowds of the curious along the way, especially at the campgrounds where we spent the nights.

During our travels, we spent hours with Nina, debating the comparative merits of American and Soviet life. Nina could be trusted to guide us through the certainties of her communal culture. She had been thoroughly indoctrinated.

For us, the debates were an exercise in futility: she believed nothing we told her.

Three days before we were to leave the country, we returned from an afternoon swim to find an ambulance with its lights flashing and rear doors flung wide open. As a pale young lady strapped to a gurney was loaded inside and whisked away, we were told that twenty-two-year-old Nina had suffered a heart disorder.

We believed then (and I remain convinced today) that it was an elaborate ruse to induce us to divulge whatever treachery we had been sent to accomplish.

Two years later, I was visiting a friend in New York City on Easter Sunday. We joined the throng in front of St. Patrick's Cathedral on Fifth Avenue, and exactly at noon, with bells pealing, a very healthy Nina Tsap appeared two feet away from me.

I froze on the spot.

For me, that instant was a true epiphany—the revealing and sudden manifestation and perception of the beliefs and fabric of our respective cultures.

"Nina!" I immediately shouted.

"Fred!" she returned. Just as quickly, two goons swept down and pulled her back into the crowd, and she disappeared. Again.

I set about finding Ken, one of my former colleagues who was studying at Columbia at the time, to discuss the strange encounter and ponder its meaning.

To my surprise, Ken said he had actually met Nina several weeks earlier, during her first days as a translator with the Ukrainian delegation to the United Nations. He asked her during lunch whether she had discovered that what we had told her about our country was true.

Nina responded by telling Ken the first thing she did on arriving in New York was to take a subway down to Wall Street and touch the walls of the Stock Exchange. When she discovered they were actually made of granite, not of cardboard as she had been taught and resolutely believed, the scales fell from her eyes.

"Yes," she said, "it was all true." And that was her epiphany.

I wrote a letter to Gerald Ford, my U.S. Congressman at

the time, to ask that travel restrictions be waived so that Nina could visit me in Ann Arbor. Ford forwarded my letter to the State Department, which arranged for a meeting.

Alas, the meeting never took place. The Soviets didn't approve.

Which brings us back to today.

There are those who, like the ministers of communism of an earlier era, preach that America is the true Satan. That you and I represent pure evil. For reasons we cannot comprehend.

Nina believed it then, from a world carefully screened from reality, just as untold numbers believe it today. Nina saw the truth for what it was as soon as she confronted the reality of our life and values.

What I find especially troubling is that the touchstone that Nina found is missing for those whose hatred is visceral, deeply believed, and unyielding.

At one time, it was the Statue of Liberty. You could touch it. You could climb within it.

Ironically, Wall Street and the buildings that inhabit it, the very site of Nina's moment of truth, have become symbols of evil for the new breed of zealots who would destroy us.

Our challenge is to find another touchstone, one that has the power to reveal truth.

We have to find it. We have to lead the world to it. We have to let them touch it. It must be something that captures the reality of our values, as expressed in our everyday life. It is a substance that will be hard to put into words that have universal meaning.

But, we must find that touchstone. And it has to be more than a Tomahawk missile.

LIBERTARIANS

A FRIEND OF MINE ONCE QUOTED A FAVORITE PHILOSOPHER of hers who said, "There are times in life when, from the imagination and not from reason, should wisdom come . . ."

I am moved to consider those among us who purposely turn away from the accepted logic or status quo to test and (re)define the boundaries of our legal and moral institutions. It can be a useful exercise, if at times somewhat ignominious.

For example, we had U.S. Constitution Ranger Ira Holborn, sixty-nine, asserting in Charlevoix District Court this week that the Constitutional guarantee of liberty means the state cannot require drivers' licenses of those who operate motor vehicles on the highways. (At least he raised the question of what the word liberty means.)

Holborn had actually cancelled his driver's license in March, putting substance to his belief, and met with the sheriff in July to file a complaint against a state police officer who had cited him for driving without a valid driver's license in another county. In apparent further defiance, Holborn drove to meet with the sheriff.

Upon leaving the sheriff's office, Holborn was promptly arrested again and charged with a misdemeanor. This week, he lost in court and will pay over $1,000 from his next three

Social Security checks for acting in defiance of the law and for the privilege of asserting his viewpoints in court.

You may dismiss Ira as illogical, but I am fascinated by him because he acts out of a conviction that most of us would not countenance.

Lyle Barkley, Bob Taylor, and Norm Olson are others from this area who come to mind. Our basic freedoms allow them to speak up and out on what they believe; and in so doing they impact our lives as well. Sometimes for the better.

It's useful to have Ira and others like him help draw the boundaries of the law, even if they only reconfirm for us what was already there. One legal source defines the quandary:

> *"Vanquished is the view that the Justices should only exercise judicial review in clear cases. In their stead is the conception that, given the 'majestic' and 'dynamic' generalities of the Constitution, jurists must inevitably 'legislate' within the wide 'interstices' of the law."*

Others who challenge the status quo are people like Nicole Perry of Bliss Township, who defied the Department of Natural Resource's (DNR) resurveying of twenty-one sections in Bliss Township, which came to be known as remonumentation or retracement. The state's survey threatened to take property that she has occupied for over thirty years.

"While I understand the surveyors' point of view that remonumentation helps them, it is based on a flawed public act because the Legislators neglected to protect the innocent people adversely affected by it. Meanwhile, ongoing retracement surveys allow government agencies like the DNR to make unilateral decisions, with no appeals process," Perry said. "The only recourse is to go to the legislators, go to court, or go to the press. Or do all three."

Well, that's the ball game, and it's frequently played out in the courtrooms, the media and lawmakers' offices, and fortunately only occasionally played out in Coeur d'Alene, Ruby Ridge, and other places where some would-be agents of change hole up.

"I believe that people who go to court to stand up for their convictions are not trying to pull the law apart," said icole, "because no one wants to live in a lawless society. They are just trying to put a human perspective to it."

How logical is that?

POTATOE

POLITICS IS AT ITS BEST WHEN IT'S INSPIRING OR DEFINITIVE or outrageously funny. Especially the latter. Let's take Dan Quayle, the former vice president who took a stab at spelling and came up with "potatoe," giving him a final "E" for effort and a media flap over his firm instruction to schoolchildren on how to spell, or misspell, the common spud.

As a Steve Martin aficionado, I occasionally taught my children the "correct" spelling of words by mispronouncing them, as in *YOSE*-mite for Yosemite, or *SEAT*-le for Seattle. My hope was that they would forever associate the proper with the improper.

This, however, turned into near disaster when my daughter, Tallie, was interviewing at Dartmouth, and was asked to name her favorite national park. She later allowed that in the nervousness of the moment, she came within a breath of responding with what would have been a major faux pas attributable to Dad. At least back then, only an education at a fine college in New Hampshire was at stake.

In politics, candidates have to be forever on guard against major miscues, lest they live with them forever. I'm not at all sure, however, that perfect blunders such as Quayle's don't endear us to the blunderers, making them human and transforming them instantly into one of us against a world of political correctness, photo opportunities, scripted speeches, and public embraces.

So it is that I propose we embrace, with a bow to Mr. Quayle, the concept of the "Michigan potatoe," a special variety to be found only in the plowfields of the Michigan north woods and recognizable only by natives attuned to the nuances of speech and meaning of local parlance.

As my first near-perfect illustration, I offer a moment in Republican Chuck Yob's brief sojourn to the area, which started with his quixotic three-day Harley Tour of the district last month to emphasize his alliance with the "real people" in his race against the sober and efficient icon of the north, Democratic Congressman Bart Stupak.

Chuck qualified for the award in a preliminary heat, by falling off his Harley and breaking an arm the day before the tour was to begin. Unfazed, Chuck announced he would battle on, though he would have to travel behind his cycling entourage in an RV.

I met Chuck on the final day of the tour. As a relative unknown, Chuck did not attract much of a crowd. I pretty much had him to myself and took the opportunity to drain the political oil out of his chassis. As a newcomer to the area myself, I lobbed a few softballs which Chuck relished, clobbering them over the fence. Obviously enjoying himself, he railed against the interference of Washington in our personal lives and cited, as a prime example, the need for local control over the selection of roads to be built and maintained.

Brass blaring, his healthy arm thumping the breeze, the maestro finally reached the high point of his performance, a single finger waving like a baton to his orchestra, signaling them to give it their all, before an unseen audience of thousands. "And, the people of Petoskey know what they need for roads, not the bureaucrats in Washington," he trumpeted. "Hell, they don't even know where AL-anson is.

They've never even *heard* of AL-anson." Wow, I thought as I reviewed the tape later, clearly Chuck's never heard of a-LAN-son either. And so, I had discovered a real Michigan potatoe; my first, right in the center of the district he hoped to cultivate.

Naturally, I chose not to report the potatoe, but rather save it for a future column. It's not my role or predeliction to make sport of people, even politicians, in a news story, but in this space anything is fair game.

Another example of the Michigan potatoe was unearthed just last weekend, at the Northern Democrats dinner in Gaylord. The guest of honor was Baroness Angela Harris of Richmond, an appointee-for-life member of the British House of Lords, the appointment itself a source of some amusement. The baroness, elegantly attired in blue and smiling mischievi-ously during her brief appearance on stage, said she was touring what might have been one of her colonies to study the politics of the natives, albeit a couple hundred years too late. With great enthusiasm, she told the 300 assembled Democrats that she "had just spent the last twenty-four hours with your congressman, Bart Stupak." There were a few immediate twitters, which escalated into a full chorus of guffaws, before she raised her arms, signaling silence.

"Well, MOST of the last twenty-four hours," she said, with gleeful satisfaction, as if that made everything proper, at least in her eyes.

Stupak, standing behind the podium, was instantly transformed into a quivering mass of mortification, if only for a few delicious seconds. Was this the end of my career? he must have thought. Fortunately he recovered with an impish grin that put everyone at ease.

Was that Michigan potatoe purposely planted? I wondered. I don't think so, but it was clearly the tastiest sidedish of the evening.

NAMES

EVERYONE KNOWS THAT POLITICIANS HAVE SHORT MEMORIES, especially when it comes to their campaign promises. But, to make up for this near-universal shortcoming, the best of the lot have an uncanny ability to recollect forever the names and faces from chance encounters so trivial that most of us would let them instantly slide into our memory abyss.

When I first arrived in Northern Michigan two years ago, I heard about the legendary memory of Pat Gagliardi, the popular Democrat who represented the 107th district in the 1980s. Pellston fire chief and local historian Randy Bricker told me how Gagliardi would park cars for the hundreds of fans attending Pellston High School football games, return them to their proper owners after the game, and recall their names years later.

So, last April, while awaiting the arrival of Congressman Bart Stupak for a fundraiser, I had a chance to see the master in action. I was talking with Larry Meier, the scourge of cormorants, when he spotted Gagliardi across the room and suggested we chat him up. Meier said he had spoken briefly to Gagliardi once five years ago on something trivial. He couldn't remember what.

As we approached, Gagliardi glanced at us, broke off his conversation, and stretched out his hand, a broad Cheshire-cat grin lighting his face. "LARRY!" he exclaimed. "It's great to see you!"

When I was introduced, Gagliardi said, "Oh, yeah. You phoned me six months ago and I never returned your call. I knew what you wanted; I just didn't want to talk about it!"

Every time I meet someone and fumble for his or her name, I remember Gagliardi's gift.

My latest embarrassment was a couple of months ago, when candidate Dick Posthumus made an early morning campaign appearance at the Perry Hotel. Republican Party District Chair Jim Erhart was there, sipping coffee with a small group of Posthumus supporters. I was keen on dispelling Erhart's impression that I was a typical left-leaning journalist, a calumny he once let slip to a colleague. So, in a loud confident voice, I proclaimed, "Hi, John. Good to see you again."

Jim didn't flinch, smiled, and gave me a cheery hello, while Scott Shackleton gently lifted my elbow and led me into a corner.

"It's Jim," Scott whispered. "Not John." Then he added, "You know, if I'm not sure about a name, I just smile and say, 'Glad to see you.'"

Good advice—had I been the least bit uncertain.

So, to apply instant damage control, I walked over to Erhart, patted him on the back and said, "Sorry, Jim. I knew better. I guess you just looked like a John."

I immediately winced, realizing I had compounded my original faux pas with an unintended double entendre and thus had planted both feet in the mire.

Fortunately, Jim has a sense of humor, and after a brief pause, we both chuckled at my unsportsmanlike behavior.

Oh, by the way, may I park your car?

DIGITAL BILLBOARDS

THEY'RE ON THEIR WAY—DIGITAL BILLBOARDS, THAT IS. Can you imagine? Cilla, my watchdog sister who lives in Charlotte, North Carolina, forwarded a column from the *Charlotte Observer*. "Thought you might enjoy this!" Cilla wrote with a dash of irony.

In the column, Urban Outlook writer Mary Newsom recounts how Lamar, a national billboard company, wants the Charlotte City Council to change its billboard ordinance so it can put up high-tech signs capable of flashing a new ad every eight seconds.

Every *eight seconds*? Yes. Every eight seconds.

Newsom quotes a Lamar spokesman as proudly telling City Council, "It's 2006. We're in a digital age."

My well-traveled colleagues tell me they have seen the digital billboards downstate, on the east side, as well as near my hometown of Grand Rapids. Actually, I believe I saw a few of them in rural Wisconsin on my way to the Oshkosh Air Show last July. They rather spoiled the show ...

To those who control the highways and byways from south to north, I say, "Puleez. Just close the door and throw away the key!"

However, digital signage would remove one objection to roadside clutter—the boredom of seeing the same sign day after day. I mean, how often can we be prompted to eat a Big Mac? Or to contemplate a furniture company's billboard promise: "Everything You Need!" Actually, I need a lot more, and may I suggest that the last thing you or I probably need is a reclining sofa-chair.

If we have to have digital billboards, why not let them entertain us? For example, why not give us movie trailers? What a fun challenge it would be to watch Tom Cruise in a *Mission Impossible* while trying to keep one eye on the road!

And the ads would be especially useful to keep kids quiet during the road construction delays that travelers must often endure.

You might think Lamar would be a bit bashful about its new products.

Not so.

Lamar's Website says the company has entered into a "new phase of growth and diversification with its recent introduction of digital billboards which allow advertisers to update their messages instantly."

The company advises that "through generations of commitment, integrity and innovation, Lamar has changed the nation's landscape while still maintaining the character of a family business."

"Changed the nation's landscape?" How's that for being candid?

I called Lamar's representatives for comment and prognostication, but they refused or were otherwise unresponsive.

I'll look closely for an instant update. We shouldn't have to wait too long . . .

Predicaments

MOOSE ON THE LOOSE

SEEING A MOOSE, EVEN IN A PHOTO, REMINDS ME OF MY favorite backwoods companion, the one who, with a nod of his head, helped Tallie and me out of total bewilderment in a Maine logging camp at 2:00 a.m. some eighteen years ago.

Young Tim Hodsdon had invited Tallie—his Dartmouth college classmate and our only daughter—for a weekend at Chairback Mountain, his parents' wilderness camp on Long Pond in the center of Maine, surrounded by thousands of square miles of logging company operations. Spooky at any time and doubly so in the middle of a star-spangled night.

Stephen King country.

Tim had written three pages of directions on yellow legal paper, which we followed on the way north from our home in Connecticut. We had no idea how far we would be traveling. After the sun had set and while we were only midway to our destination, Tallie and our son Ry, huddled underneath a blanket in the backseat, read instructions with the help of a yellow plastic flashlight.

We arrived at the logging company gatehouse long past midnight. I knocked on the door and when there was no response, I walked to the back, tapped on a pane of glass, and awoke the wizened caretaker who cracked the window and listened to my plea.

181

"Sorry to wake you," I said, "but we're trying to find Chairback Mountain Camps. I think we're close. Our directions say to ask your permission to pass through the gate and continue along the two-track."

He chuckled, pulled his trousers over his long johns, and stumbled to the pole-gate outside, which he raised with a crank and waved us through.

We continued through the thick towering forest and guided by Tim's notes, turned at shadowy boulders and ponds, only to find ourselves at dead-ends with nowhere to go. Until . . . in front of us a gigantic moose appeared, trotting proudly out of the brush exactly where Tim had predicted he would. The moose loped ahead of us, his head and shoulders washed by our headlights as he turned from side to side, checking periodically to make certain we were following him.

We did this for probably a half mile, before it stopped at the unmarked entrance to the primitive Chairback camp. Then, nodding to us to proceed along a barely discernible path, the moose bounded away and disappeared into the brush.

It seems astonishing that this, in fact, occurred. But I've confirmed my memory of the incident with my son and daughter, and with Tim, who was cooking a turkey on a spit over a wood fire when we arrived. Tim didn't miss a turn when we told him that his moose prediction had come true: I had to assume it was a usual thing. We soon spoke of other things as we wolfed down the turkey dinner, and then fell into a sound sleep.

The next day, we explored the wilderness, tipping over a canoe in an ice-cold lake and listening to the campfire tales of Shirley and Keith, Tim's mother and father. They had purchased the summer camp, which was begun in the 1860s by a one-armed Civil War soldier as a retreat for veterans.

Shirley regaled us with tales of her fights with her arch nemesis, the St. Regis Paper Company, which was intent on clear-cutting the area.

At the time of our visit, there was no electricity at the camp, and the only contact with the outside world was through a radio phone, powered by sunlight. It worked, Tim said, but not so well during the rainy period we were experiencing.

Unfortunately, our travel plans called for Tallie and Tim to return to college in New Hampshire with Ry and my wife, while I would fly to New York. Tim and Keith made many attempts to contact a private pilot on the radio phone to engage him and his float plane for a puddle jump to Bangor, the nearest airport, where I would pick up a commercial flight to LaGuardia. Each call lasted about twenty seconds before the phone expired. A succession of calls through the day succeeded in arranging for a flight at 5:00 p.m. on Sunday.

Minutes before the appointed hour, a sky full of black mushrooming clouds and lightning bolts dashed my hopes of returning to Manhattan that night; but precisely as the clock struck five, the clouds at the horizon parted, the sun shone through, and we could spot a beetle-like object hovering at the far end of the lake. It was the floatplane. When it reached the dock, I scrambled aboard and we took off. As we skimmed over the treetops on the way to Bangor, I felt myself every bit the Indiana Jones of movie legend.

CRUISIN' FOR A BRUISIN'

F EW OF YOU WILL BELIEVE IT, BUT TRUST ME, IT'S TRUE: cruising in the western Caribbean takes a lot of fortitude. When I discovered late in the year I had six days of accumulated vacation time that could not be carried over to the following year, I phoned my well-traveled companion.

"What to do?" I asked. After all, I hadn't taken a real vacation in years and was clueless. The last one I had carefully planned—a week-long fishing trip to Kabinakagami Lake in Northern Ontario—I had to cancel when my girlfriend at the time revealed through last-minute sobs that she really didn't like bugs . . . or fish . . . or wildlife.

So, this time I decided to allow my new and infinitely more adventurous companion to select the getaway. I would just tag along.

When she suggested a Caribbean cruise, I leapt with enthusiasm. On the Internet we found a tall ship sailing from St. Vincent at an attractive price and at the right time. Alas, the airfare turned out to be three times the cost of a berth.

We settled for a week-long cruise from Miami on the Norwegian Sun. It was a rousing success: plenty of exotic tropical fish, both alive and sautéed, and wildlife that swung through or soared over the steaming jungles of the Central American coast.

During off-ship excursions, we tubed through mile-long caves in Belize, snorkeled off the reefs of Grand Cayman, and skimmed through the azure waters off the Honduran island of Roatan, on what the skipper said had once been the fastest sailing ship on the Great Lakes.

And, we swam with stingrays.

"What?" you say. "Swam with the stingrays?!"

Sharks and stingrays have always been at the top of my list of things to avoid while swimming, so it was with great consternation that I agreed to an excursion to Stingray City in the waters off Grand Cayman Island.

Dozens of us were taken aboard large fishing boats to a shallow sandbar several miles from shore where hundreds of gentle stingrays the size of coffee tables flapped lazily through our legs in search of morsels of squid to suck from our hands.

Stingrays have no teeth and, so we were told, their only defense (poor things!) is a venomous barb that sticks out about a third of the way down their tails. "As long as you don't lift the rays out of the water, and you treat them with the respect they deserve, you'll have a wonderful experience," the brochure said.

Don, our sun-bronzed guide, apparently hadn't read the brochure. Cradling the rays in his arms, he cajoled us into submitting to "backrubs." He bushed the rays' velvety undersides over our posteriors while his companion Julie captured the dramatic and often hilarious reactions with her watertight camera.

After auditioning dozens of hopefuls, Don selected me for the starring role of video buffoon. Lifting a large stingray high out of the water so that its white underbelly faced me from a foot away, he encouraged me to inspect its large rectangular mouth. As I peered into its maw, the stingray unleashed a bountiful stream of seawater directly in my face, much to my astonishment and the amusement of onlookers.

Back on the boat, Julie was quick to sell us copies of the video she would stitch together during her lunch hour, as high-tech souvenirs—$40 for the VHS and $60 for the DVD version.

Julie was most enthused about selling us the DVD version, which, she said, would allow us to capture individual frames and turn them into photos.

In the end, it cost me several hundred dollars (for a DVD drive and software for my computer), in addition to the price of the cruise, airfare, and excursion, to print a single frame of the Grand Cayman stingray humiliating me.

I suppose the most positive thing I can say about the experience is that I had been stung by a stingray, if only in the pocketbook, and survived.

ACCIDENT

ONE SATURDAY EVENING, AS I WAS DRIVING AT FORTY MILES per hour through a small Northern Michigan village, minding my business, a driver two cars ahead of me braked to make a left turn, stopping suddenly to let the oncoming traffic pass.

The car ahead of me stopped, as I did; but Dan, in the car behind me, did not. BANG! He dented my trunk. He apologized profusely, seemingly at a loss as to why his brakes had failed. Although, judging from the condition of his car, he appeared to be a professional tailgater.

Because I had not taken out collision insurance on my car, I was instantly out $1,500. When I purchased the policy, I figured that if I observed the law and was not at fault, I wouldn't suffer a loss. Wrong.

I let the driver of the six-year-old, one-eyed GMC know what I thought of his driving technique. Especially as he carried on quite smugly about how the accident hadn't even scratched his car.

What bothers me is that Dan is free to roam the highways, rear-ending law-abiding citizens—like you and me—without suffering so much as a ticket. He apparently considers the highways his own private demolition derby.

I asked Dan how he dared drive at night, with his left-front headlight an obvious victim of an accident (or two or three), dating back years, judging from the accumulated rust. He responded, rather cavalierly I thought, that he simply avoided driving at night.

When I asked him for his phone number, he said he had canceled his cellular service after his previous girlfriend rang up $800 worth of calls and failed to pay for them. It was Dan's only phone, and his father, who had co-signed his insurance, turned out to be unlisted.

I wrote down his insurance information and then rushed across to the gas station to report the accident to 9-1-1.

Half an hour later, a state trooper arrived to write a report.

The trooper apologized for being tardy, reminded the kid he was responsible for maintaining his vehicle under control at all times, then let him off without a ticket. He advised me that under Michigan's no-fault system, my recovery from Dan's insurer was limited to $500. He estimated the damage to my car at about $2,000, which turned out to be right on the money—my money.

Do you have collision insurance on your vehicle? If not, you might ask yourself why. Currently twelve states and Puerto Rico have no-fault auto insurance laws. Ironically, the law in Colorado, whence I hailed seven years ago, reverted from no-fault to the tort liability system in 2003. There must have been a reason for the reversion, not that I would fare better in Colorado.

Dan said he would pay to have my car fixed, but he failed to call me Monday to confirm the deal, as promised.

If I were a gambling man, I am forced to conclude that I could either frequent a casino or try my luck on the highways. After all, it's not a matter of right and wrong out there, it's a throw of the dice. And you know what the odds are: Dan will get you—eventually.

IS THERE LIFE AFTER SHREK?

I T'S NOT THAT I DON'T LIKE MOVIES. IN FACT, BACK WHEN I was "all there" as it were, I was one of James Bond's biggest fans. After all, if brilliance is handsome, prowess has hair. Double-o-seven was licensed to kill—with good looks, a gun, and presumably a comb.

I still like Sean Connery and, for professional reasons of course, the late poet king of the road, Charles Kuralt, who, in his glory years, was short, fat, and bald. Sorry Charles.

These men, their elegance despoiled by the inevitable aging process, still knew how to present themselves with great poise, even if they were no longer working under cover, if you will, and appeared somewhat naked to young idol worshippers.

Movies have become so much of a kiddie culture these days, that I have found it almost impossible to watch a man grow old gracefully on the screen, big or small. Still, when the movie *Shrek* was released with the usual hoopla, I had my hopes. And, when the movie came and went and missed me entirely, I was not overly concerned.

Then, one evening, my friend of travel and Scrabble became unusually animated and dropped a bombshell on the way from the car to the gaming board. Referring to her thirteen-year-old son, she said, "Fred, Fred. Nick thinks you look just like Shrek!"

"Really?" I said aloud, trying to sound thrilled. While in thought I wondered if Sean Connery had become the model for some aging, but still dashing, animated spy. Had computer-aided artists polished his dome with their Wacom sticks? Could this be the first recognition from Nick, who had heretofore barely acknowledged that I existed, of my worth as a human being?

"Really," she said, and then pertly insisted I watch the recently released video to see for myself.

So I did; amongst others. A few minutes worth.

In an instant, my entire self-image was shattered beyond redemption. For those of you who don't already know, the enormously popular Shrek is best described as a man-sized, leathery green egg with stubby twigs for ears, bulbous eyes, and a fat mouth. And not one strand of hair.

And I, as the new-age Humpty Dumpty, had taken a great fall.

As you might expect, a moment of profound silence followed Shrek's grand entrance, as everyone waited for the effect to be revealed. Seeing that I was far from convinced—in fact, I was in the classic state of denial, almost catatonic with disbelief—my friend again pressed the fast-forward button.

"Wait, wait. Let me find the part where you look JUST like Shrek," she said, sensing she may have inflicted a mortal wound and offering the celluloid equivalent of mouth-to-mouth resuscitation.

"Stop. Stop. Here's the part!" exclaimed Nick, squirming on the sofa, his eyes shining with glee.

The fat green egg-man has entered the castle grounds and is gesticulating wildly, eyes popping, twiggy ears twirling, gut bulging, dancing around on spindly legs, pronouncing his mission to save the world from evil-doers. An absolute fool that Shakespeare himself would have been proud of.

"That's you! That's YOU!" Nick shouted. Everyone, an

audience of five, doubled over in laughter, pointing at me before losing all control and clasping their hands to their shaking bellies.

It must be true, I thought. How can anyone so utterly wrong be so utterly convinced?

On the other hand, maybe he's not wrong, and if so, I have my rights. If Shrek and I are like two peas in a pod, my pod obviously came first. The egg came after the chicken. He's the clone, not me. What fun to have my day in court.

Later that night, my friend solemnly announced that we had entered Phase Two of our relationship. She wasn't exactly sure how to describe Phase Two; but she surely had it right, it WAS a new phase.

If I was now Shrek, I certainly had crossed a line and was being herded by an electronic prod into life's corral of "everyone else," the billions of us who appear to the more fortunate as ordinary leather-green eggs.

About to feel sorry for my passing, I suddenly recalled the enormous red-faced Irishman who thirty-five years ago managed our apartment building in Ann Arbor and refused to authorize the name we had chosen for the seafood shop we were about to open there—The Pink Pig—thinking we were dishonoring HIM!

My then-wife glibly explained that she was truly honoring ME, because of what I looked like after a day in the sun. He relented. I didn't.

If we were doing it over again, I expect we would have named the store Shrek's Lobsters and Clams and made millions.

A man born before his time, I am. Born before my time.

Shrek—fat, green, and bald—can apparently sell himself to anyone. Except me.

I still have a healthy fringe of the curly, and I refuse to go quietly into the night.

THE LAST COMB-OVER

Ain't no finer rig, I'm a-thinkin', than that shiny little
surrey with the fringe on the top.
from "Oklahoma!" by Rodgers and Hammerstein

MOM OFTEN REPEATED AN OLD ADAGE THAT WENT SOME-thing like this: "Up to the age of forty, you have the face you're born with. After that, you have the face you deserve."

I guess it was a way of preparing her boys to accept the ultimate reality of manhood, while at the same time cleverly avoiding genetic responsibility for hair loss and other potentially fatal maladies.

It was, in fact, on my fortieth birthday that I swallowed my pride (on the advice of a friend) and celebrated the epochal transition with a stark initiation into the world of the visually circumscribed, a day I will forever remember as "The Last Comb-Over."

Earlier I suspected my moment of truth was rapidly approaching when a British colleague, suitably blessed with abundant hair that swept over his forehead and nearly into his eyes, instigated a ritual at the morning news conference in New York. As I walked through the door each morning, he would jump to attention, salute, lift his chin high in the air, click his heels, and shout: "Hair count!" The jest invariably raised guffaws from the others, many of them similarly challenged.

Today, I wonder if I made the right choice.

Judging from the unqualified success of Carl Levin, whose comb-over and vote count top all challengers, I too might have been a U.S. senator had I followed his path. The senator, his reading glasses perched on the tip of his nose, has been prodded mercilessly by hirsute pretenders who openly mimic the eloquence of his signature hair by sweeping their own locks upward and over and allowing their glasses to slide precariously down the nasal ridge.

As amusing as the impersonations might be, you really can't argue with success, even if it is—in one important respect—that of a "cockeyed optimist." After all, the image of the avuncular politician is surely one of the main components of his lasting popularity.

I grew up accepting the unchallenged twentieth-century scientific doctrine that a man's hairline was gifted by his maternal grandfather. Dad, a handsome hair-shy obstetrician, loved to assure me that the bounteous crop of hair atop Grandpa Bertsch was my just inheritance.

I believed him. As a high-school senior, I fashioned my image after Elvis, pampering a long spit curl that grew out of my head like the pride of a unicorn.

The maternal grandfather's legacy became an article of faith between Dad and me, albeit one that was challenged with each passing year—and shampoo. As Dad's belief in textbook science slowly evaporated, he subscribed to a new theory that hair loss could be reduced by mercilessly scrubbing down one's dome in the shower.

When he gave me a bristle brush for Christmas, I knew my days as a matinee idol were numbered and my promised inheritance utterly lost. I admired his persistence; but he might as well have signed me up for a year's worth of Avacor.

Over the years, I've met others who simply refuse to yield to reality, my favorite being Bernd Debusmann, an ace Reuters reporter who sashayed around the world with his Teleram, a prototype computer of the early '80s with a modem so slow you could count the characters as they were squeezed into the phone line.

Bernd, a German by birth, was both an eccentric creature of habit and a flamboyant adventurer who survived gunshot wounds in Lebanon and the loss of a thumb while skydiving.

After I had assumed the mantel of technical director of the editorial wing of Reuters, Bernd would call me from the jungles of South America and the deserts of Asia to declare his everlasting love for his ponderous machine and beg special dispensation from my periodic edicts commanding all journalists to master and carry the latest in laptops.

Bernd was oblivious of the ridiculousness of his comb-over, and I loved him for it. But then, I'm a nostalgic sap who has been brought to tears by Nellie Forbush, the Navy nurse in the Broadway musical *South Pacific*, who offered her own comb-over excuse for failing to see the folly of falling hopelessly in love with a much older man:

"I'm only a cockeyed optimist," she sang, "and I can't get it into my head."

If only Oscar Hammerstein had written *onto* instead of *into*, he might well have penned the eternal lament of follicular challenged men everywhere.

MUGGED IN MICHIGAN

IT WAS A CLEAR SPRING NIGHT ON 43RD STREET NEAR GRAND Central Station. I had just finished the evening shift on the World Desk at the Associated Press. I had a full half-hour to walk the nine short blocks that separated Rockefeller Center from Grand Central before catching the 12:35 a.m. home to Connecticut. I often took a different route to the station to drink in the exotic pleasures of New York City at night.

Suddenly, a block from the floodlit entrance to Grand Central, I was surrounded by a dozen young punks, their knives flashing, dancing a full circle around me, and demanding my wallet, watch, and whatever other valuables they thought I might be carrying or wearing.

Taunting me with twisting blades that darted too close to my neck, they took turns shouting phrases they had clearly used before, like "Hey mon, your money. We know you have it. All of it." The "or else" was clearly implied.

In return for my life, the dancing dozen settled for the only thing of value I had on or about me—a triangular platinum watch Dad gave me as a college graduation present. It wasn't much, but it gave me a lease on life. And, I'm sure Dad would have been happy I used it as a "Get Out of Hell Free" card.

When I entered Grand Central, I quickly approached two police officers who were lolling about and pointed to the gang that was still visible under the street lamps as they skipped west along 43rd Street. "Officers," I recall saying in a rush. "I was just mugged by those guys. You can still catch them."

The policemen looked at me oddly, as though I was a lunatic, threw up their hands, and said it was really none of their business. Their duties were confined to ensuring the safety of those using Grand Central.

Before catching my train, I had a minute or so to call the precinct police, who put me on a lengthy hold. Finally, an officer reluctantly took my name and phone number and opened an incident report. I told him I had to leave.

The next day, having discovered I was a newsman, a public relations officer for the city took a heightened interest in the case, and asked me to come down to the station to look through mug books. But it came to nothing. I discovered that all crooks look alike.

That was at least twenty years ago, and I don't pretend that being mugged in New York City is anything other than a rite of initiation. Still, when I eventually moved to Northern Michigan, I didn't expect to face down another group of like-minded thieves—until I opened by phone bill and found AT&T demanding a king's ransom for a single eighty-minute phone call to "Saltstmari, ON", at 10:48 p.m. on a Friday in August.

Oh sure. It was a great phone call. You might as well know it was to a blind date, whose first words on meeting me were, "You're a little short, aren't you?" and then let me know that despite an afternoon of polishing, the cleanliness of my car was not up to her standards.

Well, I guess she wasn't blind after all, was she?

She was summarily dismissed. The disappointment was mutual.

But the most damaging insult in this episode was the phone company's ransom, which I calculated at eighty-three cents a minute—exactly SIX TIMES the rate I would have been charged if my call had been to a blind date in Sault Ste. Marie, MICHIGAN, just over an international border that added no measurable distance to the length of wire carrying my words.

Certain that a mistake had been made, I braved AT&T's maze of automated customer service instructions, which kept me from a live human for a period that must be calculated in terms of "forever less a day" rather than the usual method of estimating time in minutes.

Clearly AT&T believes that most customers, confronted by a wall of endless instruction and useless information about their Website, will hang up in frustration.

Not me. I stayed the course, and when I finally made a human connection and asked politely about the outrageous charge, I was ushered into a world of double-speak and unparalleled ignorance.

The following Saturday, I received a phone call from a company representative who listened politely, sympathized even, but then avowed that my complaint should be registered with the Federal Communications Commission (FCC), which she said sets the rates for international calls.

That led me to make yet another mistake—calling the FCC to verify the information AT&T had conveyed to me. After all, wasn't there a free trade agreement in place between our two countries?

Oh, the pain I caused!

The way everyone at the FCC scurried for cover, you would have thought I was Slim Pickens waving my cowboy hat as I rode a nuclear warhead marked "The Big Question." I had to go through at least five people over three days before I found an FCC lawyer, who on the condition I would not divulge his name, offered to cite what he believed to be the law on the subject. In hushed tones, he told me that the FCC had long ago given up setting international phone rates, and that with deregulation, the phone companies in a competitive market such as Canada/U.S. could charge whatever the market would bear. The FCC was simply not involved.

"You mean, AT&T lied to me?" I asked in pretended incredulity.

"I'll leave that for you to characterize," he deadpanned.

When I called AT&T back, in hopes of finding a corporate spokesman to sort it all out, the young lady I spoke with said she did not know where company headquarters was located—she believed it was New Jersey or Pennsylvania— and the best she could do would be to have someone call me back the next day.

It's already been several days, and I'm still waiting! I want to tell them I'm wearing a cheap Casio watch I'd be willing to give them in return for another few days on earth.

ROOT ROT TRUMPS ROOT CHAKRA

*I found it interesting that you're so concerned about
your Root Chakra! What about mine? (I must have
been asleep when they explained it all at college).*
Letter to a friend

FOUND THE DEFINITION OF *ROOT CHAKRA* ON THE WEB. FOR
those of you not yet in tune, *Root Chakra* is the center of
physical energy and vitality, the energy to be engaged
with the physical world and, thereby, succeed in business or
material possessions. Throughout the ancient world in historical and mythological stories, Root Chakra has been
depicted as a dragon or a snake.

There are certain recommended practices for "rooting" or
"grounding" purposes, such as dancing, going barefoot,
cleaning house, cooking, and, for good measure, hugging a
tree and taking care of houseplants.

All that's good advice and information, but here is the
true essence of Root Chakra that all of us will find appealing:

"When the energies or vibrations from two people's chakras
are mixed, the following takes place: The light from the one
chakra affects the light from the other chakra, and these light
waves are mixed in a way so they create different figures.

"The figures created by the light waves from the chakras become more beautiful, the more love there is between the parties."

Now, all that sounded pretty intriguing, so I shed my shoes, cleaned house, and baked stuffed eggplant. And, when I took care of Mom's plant yesterday, I felt I had definitely entered the chakra-plus column. Let me tell you about it.

The plant of which I speak was a peace lily that Mom, an amazingly sharp ninety-one, had over-watered and, thus, caused a near deadly case of root rot. Ever hear of it? It's nothing like Root Chakra, believe me. Root rot produces the absolutely worst smell that can happen on this Earth.

Mom called me in a panic when she first got wind of it as she passed by the deceptively lovely plant sitting by the window. Brother Dave was due to arrive at any minute, with his socially prominent friends from Leland, and she was worried that they would get a whiff of the rot and all would be lost. She would be forever condemned and threatened to take her own life. What could I do?

I told her that as the plant had sat benignly in her apartment since it was gifted to her six months ago, it would probably make it through the pending visitation without causing serious embarrassment. I promised to come over and remove it after the guests had departed.

However, on entering Mom's apartment that evening, I had to toss aside my casual attitude, for there she was, waving a heavily perfumed handkerchief in great circles over the plant, as if blessing it.

Like Root Chakra, the two aromas together were more powerful than the sum of the parts, so I quickly opened the sliding glass door to the balcony in hopes a hurricane would blow through while I somehow got rid of the plant.

The plant's base was wrapped in foil, which had collected every drop of water that Mom had poured into it over months of loving care. Touching the bulging foil was like depressing a boil, and I feared it would burst a leak as I ushered it across the carpet to the kitchen sink for further examination. Had it done so, Mom would have to move out of her apartment to give fumigators the opportunity to address the issue.(I was reminded of the song that asked, when everything goes south, "Who ya gonna call? Ghostbusters!" Right! But, would they be so brave to confront the root rot?)

I wrapped the base of the plant in layers of garbage bags and then recalled that freedom and fresh air were four floors down and a swift lock-kneed sprint away. I decided to lance the boil at the kitchen sink.

Holding my nose with one hand and closing my eyes, I poked the foil with a knife. What issued forth was semi-liquid gaseous goo of the kind that surely circulates only through the rivers of Hades. I again wrapped the plant in protective layers of plastic and whisked it to my car, where I put it in the passenger seat so that I could threaten it with terminal mayhem on the way home if it misbehaved.

Once safely parked, I decided to leave the plant outside for the night, exposing the outside world to the smell rather than foul the interior of my dwelling. And, lo! When I awakened the following morning, the odor had mercifully departed! The gas had passed!

I took the carcass to a florist, where a young woman acknowledged that plants can indeed turn into organs of mass destruction and offered to replant it for five dollars. This I agreed to, but a week later she called to tell me the smell was terminal and I should replace the original, which was about to be cremated.

The price of thirty-one dollars for a new sweet-smelling peace lily was the best investment ever, and I made Mom promise to water it sparingly, lest she over-indulge again.

The only thing left for me now is to find a proper tree to hug so that I can realize the promise that "figures created by the light waves from the chakras will now become more beautiful and create lots of love between the parties."

PROCRASTINATION

A LITTLE PROCRASTINATION CAN PAY ENORMOUS DIVIDENDS. I know that's true when I review the downward spiral of my 401(k) and calculate how much money I've saved by not raising my contribution to the limit, as I vowed to do many times over the past year or so.

I also think of this when I recall the many dentists who, over half a lifetime, have suggested my remaining wisdom teeth be removed—by them, of course—to avoid difficulties "later in life."

Now, "later in life" is the key phrase for a guy like me. That's a long way off for someone on the waning cusp of middle age. I still have time, I keep telling myself.

But, my case for the power of positive procrastination rests on the earnest recommendation of Bob, the vaunted Steamboat Springs, Colorado, mechanic and choice of everyone at the Today, the town's tabloid newspaper where I spent a few months before migrating to Northern Michigan.

Those of us who drive aging vehicles know how vulnerable we are to mechanics' casual observations, especially mechanics in white uniforms who have spent a moment or two in or under our cars.

"Just say 'Ah'," they might as well be saying, as we lift the hood and beg for a shot of Novocain.

Bob only had to look at the odometer to note that my 1994 Explorer, at 160,000 miles, had entered the "later in life" stage and was in need of some serious transmission work.

Well, that was 120,000 miles ago. Finally, after three years of procrastination and a growing number of heart-stopping pauses at intersections waiting for the gears to engage, I decided it was time to heed Bob's advice.

In moments of doubt, I have asked myself whether Bob was a con artist looking for a mark; a skilled practitioner of the mechanical arts; or a born-again Nostradamus, the sixteenth-century astrologer and physician whose vague prophecies are said to have predicted World War II. In any event, by choosing to procrastinate, I saved myself the price of a new transmission and possibly that of a new car.

Have you ever considered the list of things that have been recommended to you by experts—but you never got around to doing? A tummy tuck or nose bob or new head of hair or new pair of shoes?

I hesitate to mention the new pair of shoes because my current pair has lasted over two years. In my opinion, despite their appearance, they still have a lot of life left in them. But Mom has gifted me shoe money, $30 for Christmas and another $30 for my birthday, so I am about a third of the way to the price of what I really deserve—a pair of Eccos, the ultimate in foot comfort.

I have promised myself to buy the shoes—as soon as I've paid for the transmission.

CONSUMER PROTECTIONISM

*At no time was there ever any intent or attempt to 'lie',
deceive or defraud Mr. Gray as set forth in his
rather nasty letters.*
Kim Gasior, VP, Jerry Baker, America's Master Gardener

I ONLY TURN NASTY WHEN I FEEL I'M BEING HAD BY AN UNFOR-tunate and obvious marketing ploy. Such as the one that began last June . . .

There I was on a sunny Saturday morning, looking over the large lawn I had agreed to maintain as part of my obligations under the lease on my new (to me) apartment.

I was listening to the radio broadcast of Jerry Baker, author of some fifty books, who bills himself grandiosely as "America's Master Gardener."

Jerry is the guy who recommends soaking grass seed in a mixture of dishwashing liquid and Epsom salts in a gallon of weak tea (use a twice-used bag) water, and leaving it all on the driveway to dry. Or, adding a drop of whiskey to ammonia and another gallon of weak tea to energize plants. Or drizzling antiseptic mouthwash into a mixture of household solutions to make a cure for fusarium blight, whatever that may be.

I call him Jerry instead of something more formal because he looks like my beloved Uncle Howard, upon whose polished dome weeds would never grow. And besides, you have to admire what might be called in other circles the guy's chutzpah.

To me, Jerry combines the audacity of Professor Harold Hill, the con man in *The Music Man*, with the pretended "aw-shucks" modesty of a Smoky Mountain hayseed. I ask myself, why does the image of Martha Stewart smoking a corncob pipe come to mind?

Still, I have to like Jerry, despite my nasty letters to him, Michigan Attorney General Michael Cox, and the state's Consumer Protection Agency.

On that summer morning, Jerry was carrying on about what a deal he had for me: he would send me six months' worth of his "On The Garden Line" newsletter (three copies) absolutely free and, after sampling it, I could subscribe for about $20 a year. Now, I usually don't succumb to over-the-air deals; but I figured I didn't have anything to lose. I called the 800 number and signed up.

You can imagine my surprise when, a few days later, I received my first free issue with an "INVOICE" for $22.88 due July 1.

Outraged, I wrote Jerry and asked him to cancel his mailings to me. "Contrary to your stated policy, I received a bill with my very first issue of the newsletter. I believe this to be dishonest advertising, however valuable the newsletter may be," I wrote. "You should be ashamed of your blatant dishonesty and I believe you should be prosecuted as well. I am forwarding a copy of this letter to the Michigan Department of Consumer Protection."

My letter, and a copy forwarded by the AG's office, apparently got to Jerry's marketing and legal staff about the same time. On November 1, they wrote the Consumer Protection

Agency, with a copy to me, to explain that the invoice was "if he wanted to continue the subscription for another year."

My goodness! How thoughtful! It only "appeared" to be an invoice for the free newsletters, I thought. How many others would make the same assumption and simply pay up?

The trouble for Jerry was that back in July, only days after I received the first invoice, I received the second free newsletter and an "INVOICE" stating that this one was "PAST DUE! REMIT BY July 22"—months before the free trial expired. Now really, how could the charge for a free mailing be past due?

Their November letter prompted me to write a second letter, this one admittedly nastier than the first. It was met by a response dated December 5 that was quite insulting—but in the end they caved.

"Based on some customer comments along the lines of Mr. Gray's complaint about the 'past due' language contained in the second invoice, we decided to modify our mailings in late July of this year.

"During the free subscription period, the customer receives the exact same documentation regarding their free issues, but we have changed the word 'invoice' to 'subscription acknowledgment,' and removed any references to 'past due.'"

So, why didn't they admit in their November 5th letter that they had already made the change in July?

Anyway, Jerry's legal team thought it was my fault for not reading closely the small print "Dear Subscriber" letter under the invoice that explained the whole thing.

"We are unaware of any respondent to our free trial subscription that could not read or understand the language of our enclosure letters, clearly explaining that the amounts were due if, and only if, the person desired to continue the subscription beyond the free trial period."

Right. Sure. I'm the moron, and I rest my case.

EXERCISE

I ATE A SANDWICH THE OTHER NIGHT. THAT'S RIGHT. A WHOLE sandwich. It was, shall we say, a memorable Reubenesque moment.

Under the blast of the service station microwave, the gooey Swiss cheese cemented two thin slices of corned beef to a gob of sauerkraut, the excess oozing out of the slabs of Ciabatta toast onto my fingertips with an occasional dribble falling onto my shiny parka.

Forgive my blather. It was my first sandwich in months. And it was delicious.

It was also the first chink in the armor of my six-month regime of exercise and diet, designed to bring me back into favor with the health charts and their keepers.

I was initially inspired to take action by our governor, who is constantly reminding us that Michiganders top the list of the nation's obese; by my sister Cilla, who has whipped North Carolinians into shape with her televised exercise programs; and by my doctor.

It was the latter who, a month or so ago, greeted my visit with a broad grin and glad hand.

"You are my success story of the day," he said, waving the results of my blood test in the air. "Since your last visit, you have cut your cholesterol levels in half, and your glucose is down as well."

Good news from doctors and dentists is rare, so I basked in the glow of what, for me, was a blessed event.

When I told him of my program of exercise at the college, under the tutelage of a personal trainer, he said that alone most likely accounted for my return to physical favor. Then, he fired up his laptop and plunked in a few figures from the test.

"You'll be happy to know, you now have a one in ten chance of dying before the age of eighty," I recall him saying, as if he had just discovered the fountain of youth. "With your previous test, your chances were two in ten."

Hmm. Fifteen more years to live it up.

"Of course, we don't give guarantees," he smiled.

That's how I heard it, anyway.

And so, I offer you a tip: The track and exercise room at local community college are terrific, and use of them is but pennies a day—the best deal in town. Anyone can enroll and show up at any time, as often and for as long as inspiration lasts. And, you do your thing, at your own pace.

And, the gym is fun! It is the local watering hole, paid for with tax dollars. You'll see everyone there: ordinary citizens interspersed with judges, commissioners, planners, academics, beauties, and behemoths. It's hard to distinguish rank and waistline when all are in sweats.

There's delicious gossip and local history as you chat with your fellow circuit riders, legs churning the pedals of stationary bicycles or arms pumping adjustable slabs of iron. Couples walk together around the tenth-mile loop, often in connubial silence; but more often in "After you, Alphonse" fashion, deciding whether either can go yet another lap. Singles are usually on a cell phone or listening to a Walkman.

The walkers and runners keep their eyes on the denizens of the exercise room, wondering no doubt if their time is better spent on the machines. I know this because friends acknowledge me with furtive expressions, maybe a waggle of a finger or a nod of a head, as they make their rounds. It's tough responding when 150 pounds of iron commands your attention, but they know I see them.

So, I am committed and allow myself a Reuben twice a year.

IMPULSE

An "irresistible impulse" is recognized as a defense to crime in Michigan, even if the defendant had been able to comprehend the nature and consequences of his act, and to know that it was wrong.

from *Anatomy of a Murder* by Robert Traver

I F WE ARE HONEST, WE MUST ALL ADMIT TO HARBORING A slightly sinister self inside our otherwise respectable personae. My self-realization began with the discovery at a tender age that appearances aren't all they seem and can be mischievously altered to achieve delicious ends. Take the cake in the fridge, for example. In a whole lifetime, you only get a single shot at one—and, therefore, you have to make it count.

And so it was, that on a fateful afternoon, at an age when I barely knew right from wrong but certainly knew cake from castor oil, I opened the refrigerator door and found a gleaming three-layer cake and felt an overwhelming challenge to my creativity and hunger.

I was taken by an "irresistible impulse," which I would later learn is a legal defense to the most heinous of crimes, including cake homicide.

I spent the better part of the afternoon carving out the interior layers of the cake, eating the evidence while making certain the exterior remained intact. When I heard Mom's car in the driveway, I quickly sealed the opening and returned it to the fridge.

In retrospect, it was an achievement no less momentous than prisoners of war tunneling under Stalag 17. I remember feeling a surge of pride as I tiptoed quickly to my basement bedroom, fully sated, to innocently resume my studies.

Unfortunately for my well-being, Mom had planned to entertain the bridge crowd that night, and I listened to the unfolding of events upstairs with trepidation and growing horror. As the games drew to a close and the hubbub of social chatter grew louder, I heard Mom open and close the refrigerator door and walk to the dining room, where crystal plates had been stacked earlier in the day alongside a sparkling array of silver forks and a polished coffee urn.

There was a long pause in conversation as the guests admired the artistry invested in the cake, and then I heard a loud gasp and the dreaded phrase, "Oh, Freddie!"

I knew Mom had just discovered the corpse. She had, with a single slice, cut into the hollow cake, causing it to implode into a puddle of frosting and little else.

There was a penalty to pay, of course, but the success of my deviltry has been a hallmark of my youth and a source of constant inspiration . . .

Like last weekend.

My friend and I had escaped to the hamlet of Big Bay, some twenty miles west of Marquette, where a homicide at the Lumberjack Saloon fifty years ago inspired Robert Traver to write the best selling novel *Anatomy of a Murder*, that was later a cinematic vehicle for Jimmy Stewart and a cast of notables.

We checked in at the Thunder Bay Inn, where the bar

scenes were filmed, and then walked down the road to the Lumberjack, primarily to be able to tell friends that we had visited the very spot where the murder occurred. The Lumberjack was dark and full of hangdog characters of dubious means who paid scant attention to each other, let alone to the yellowed and barely readable newspapers that hung from the walls and recounted the murder and its celebrated aftermath.

Not especially hungry but feeling obliged to pay our way, we ordered an appetizer plate that turned out to be a giant mound of vegetables, mostly green peppers and onions, spread over tortilla chips and melted cheese. We could only make our way through half of it, so we took away the rest in a container for later.

The following morning, as my companion showered endlessly down the hall and I reviewed selected scenes from the video of *Anatomy*, I was overtaken by an irresistible impulse and reached for the plastic container of veggies that that had been ours to share.

I mentally divided the feast in half, fully intending to share the rest with my friend; but when she hadn't returned in a respectable time, I began to carve away at what was left, much as I had the cake of yesteryear.

The mound of veggies grew smaller and smaller the longer she stayed away, and when the green peppers and I had been alone together for over an hour, there was little left but the container, which I hid in the wastebasket.

When she finally returned, I casually suggested that we might have breakfast. "Although I am not particularly hungry," I added, "and, in any event, it is rather late for a morning meal." She agreed, so we spent the day exploring and taking in the autumn colors.

When at last we ended up in St. Ignace for a late dinner, she said she was famished and wondered how I could have made it through the entire day without eating. At that point I felt a confession was in order. I fessed up to having polished off the entire plate of veggies while she showered. She laughed loudly and shook her head.

"The devil made you do it!" she exclaimed.

"No. It was just an irresistible impulse," I said sheepishly in self-defense, knowing that Jimmy Stewart and Robert Traver, at least, would have understood.

SEARS

THERE WERE ONLY A COUPLE THINGS LEFT TO DO BEFORE CLOS-ing the cottage for the winter. One was to store the canoe at Ryde's Marina in Ponshewaing; the other was to have the Sears guy inspect the gas stove. The latter was a big deal, first because last year Cilla had replaced the ancient stove that had a habit of falling to pieces whenever the oven door was opened. Or looked at. No one ever baked a second pie in that stove, believe me! You know, "once burned, twice shy."

So, a week in advance, Cilla, from her home in Charlotte, North Carolina, made an appointment for the inspection, after getting my assurance that I would open the cottage for the Sears man the following Friday afternoon.

She phoned the 800 number on the service contract and made the arrangements. I called later to request they phone me with a two-hour advance warning, which they agreed to do on the day of the appointment.

When Friday rolled around, there was a call on the answering machine from someone who sounded like he was already in the oven, mumbling something entirely unintelligible. I called Sears to ask what was going on. They checked and said the repairman had called from his last appointment of the day, was "on his way," and would call me within a few minutes.

Ten minutes later, without having received the promised

call, I decided to make the forty-five-minute drive to the cottage. When I arrived, there was no Sears man waiting, so I called the 800 number to advise the service that at least I had arrived. Five different receptionists disconnected me before one stayed on the line long enough to tell me—again—that the repairman had just completed his next-to-last inspection of the day and was headed for Mackinaw City. He was leaving Charlotte that moment, she said.

"Charlotte?" I exclaimed. "Charlotte's near Lansing. That's at least three hours away. He'll never be here by five o'clock."

"Oh, I assure you he will," she said.

I hung up. And then it struck me. Charlotte as in *North Carolina*, not Michigan. And to think the poor repairman was now headed out for Mackinaw City, which he likely had a hard time finding on the map. I had this marvelous vision of a Sears van skimming the highway at 600 miles per hour, horn blasting, wheels churning, in a frantic effort to arrive on time.

I made my umpteenth free call to Sears to explain the basics of high school geography, and suggested that the poor repairman be called off the job. I also suggested that if the "free inspection" was not a ruse to allow Sears to void the warranty, we could reschedule the appointment for the following Friday, on the condition that they would notify me two hours in advance of the appointment, which should be his *last* of the day. The scheduler agreed, and I made my arrangements.

Friday came, and when I returned to the office from a morning meeting, there was a message from the local repairman, explaining cheerfully that I was his first appointment of the day and he would be at the cottage shortly.

I called Sears, told them I had given up and would call next summer for an appointment, when the cottage was occupied.

The following day I drove to the cottage and found a sticker on the cottage door. It read: "Sorry we missed you . . . We were here at 9:40 a.m."

INTOLERANCE

I WAS FIRST INTRODUCED TO THE OVERZEALOUS WHEN MY SON Ryan, in his last day as a high school senior, stood like the man we had brought him up to be and took responsibility for the class prank: spinning a web of string in the halls of his beloved school.

Ryan told the local police investigating the hilarity that as class president, he would cooperate with them fully in an attempt to absolve his classmates from any further investigation that might jeopardize their future and the memory of his class. For his honesty, Ryan was dragged to the police station and came close to being charged with a criminal misdemeanor, a possibility that was thwarted only when our attorney convinced the prosecutor to consider the devastation a formal charge would bring to our son's budding career.

That frightful episode cost us $500 in attorney's fees and produced a vale of tears, but the legal persuasion ensured that Ryan would be able to pursue the college education he had earned through years of earnest study and leadership. It also taught us that the price of honest admission of any misdeed, however slight, may be high indeed.

That was some twelve years ago; but the danger of overzealousness was emphasized recently by a string of events that ended in profound and ironic injustice to a young woman of character and proven talent.

It began six months ago when Ashley (not her real name), the thirty-year-old daughter of a friend and a model employee with exemplary reviews at a large firm in the health support industry, sought to console a colleague who was prone to fits of depression verging on the suicidal. Ashley went to her colleague's home on a Saturday evening with a mutual friend, also employed by the same firm, and the three listened to music and talked about life and its challenges.

Late in the evening, the troubled friend brought out a vial of cocaine and proceeded to use it. Ashley, out of curiosity and with enormous regret today, touched the white powder with the tip of her pinky and tasted it in the manner we have all seen TV detectives do during an investigation at a crime scene; and left in disgust.

The following Wednesday, the human resources manager informed Ashley that, in the course of an investigation of another incident, it was alleged that she was seen "using cocaine" at an employee's house. He asked her to take a drug test, which she readily agreed to.

"I certainly did not think that the tiny taste that I took of the cocaine constituted drug use and I was certain that any test would return a negative result," she later wrote to the CEO of the company.

During the interview, however, Ashley made the fatal admission that she had run her pinky along the mirror and tasted the cocaine.

"It was my belief at the time that my employer would respect my honesty and integrity in admitting I tasted the drug rather than have the test come back positive after my assertion that I had not used the drug," she wrote.

Twenty-five minutes later, Ashley was abruptly terminated

on grounds that no exceptions could be made to the company's zero-tolerance policy on drug use, and was told a drug test was no longer necessary because of her admission.

Ashley submitted to a drug test at her own expense the following day, and the results proved negative.

"I would think that the spirit of any drug policy would be to identify employees whose work is being affected by drug use or to prohibit drug use on company premises, not to indiscriminately dismiss quality employees for making one error in judgment outside the workplace," she wrote in her futile plea for justice. "I was not and am not a drug user. I made a mistake and was punished for admitting it," she wrote.

Ashley noted that had she lied and waited for the results of the drug screen, she would still have her job—as do the other two who attended the Saturday evening session.

But, the Midwestern state in which the events took place allows companies to terminate employees at will—for any reason. And Ashley's company refused to reconsider her case despite the private admission of high-level managers that she had been dealt a severe injustice.

Ashley looked for another job for the next six months, during which she was forced by lack of income to move out of her apartment and in with her mother, while state officials refused to grant her unemployment on grounds she was an alleged drug user.

A professor of employment law at a top university told Ashley her case was one he would use to illustrate the injustice wrought by a policy of sub-zero tolerance in an at-will state, and advised her to seek legal counsel from one of his former students.

The final irony occurred when a headhunter, oblivious of the facts in Ashley's case, called her and asked if she would be interested in a position—her position—at the company that had terminated her.

"As a result of a zero-tolerance policy without exceptions, a very talented employee lost her job for nothing more than making one mistake and being, perhaps, naively honest. And I have been branded a drug user amongst those who once respected me. The entire situation has been a rather bitter learning experience," she concluded.

Ashley eventually found employment, but her experience should be fair warning to everyone of the possible consequences of what might appear to be an inconsequential event.

Like spinning a web of string in high school hallways on graduation day.

THE PRESS

THE POWER OF THE PRESS, AT THE SMALLEST AND MOST intimate level, was made painfully apparent to me some twenty-five years ago, when I flew home to Grand Rapids from Connecticut to attend my father's funeral. At the time, I had what to me was an exalted position on the cables desk with the Associated Press (AP) in Rockefeller Center, editing incoming copy from correspondents around the world for U.S. newspapers, including the daily dispatches from Vietnam.

Mom was naturally on edge over Dad's death, the funeral arrangements, and the large numbers of friends and relatives who had converged to attend the services. Although she was outwardly in self-control and as organized as one can be in such circumstances, I felt especially concerned when Mom took me aside and pointed with considerable distress to a copy of the *Grand Rapids Press*.

"They used the AP story on your father, instead of the obituary I so carefully prepared," she said. "Can you explain to me why?"

I read the AP story and realized with surprise that it had been written with the best intentions by my friends on the cables desk in New York, from their recollection of casual conversations we had had while getting to know one another. But, they got a number of things wrong, including an assertion that Dad, an obstetrician/gynecologist, had delivered all four of the children of then President Gerald R. Ford and his wife, Betty—not just Susan Ford, as was in fact the case.

"How could this happen?" Mom asked in tears. I felt a crushing responsibility for having caused her pain. And anger at the local paper for having chosen to print the AP story rather than Mom's much more interesting and accurate account, and at my colleagues for having the audacity to write such a story based on a recollection of facts without thoroughly checking them.

Ironically, the foreign editor of the AP at the time told every newcomer to the desk: "I never want to hear you try to explain a mistake you let go by, with 'That's the way it came in.'" We normally lived by that firm instruction. Perhaps my friends thought they could make an exception for "That's the way we remembered it."

None of us in the press can claim to be above reproach, which is why we have a section reserved for corrections. But, we must and do work hard to keep the utilization of that space to a minimum, because the damage to the parties involved, including the newspaper, is hard to repair.

Right, Mom?

WHITEFISH

I FELT INSPIRED AS I APPROACHED CHARLEVOIX ON MY WAY TO the Cherry Capital Airport in Traverse City, for my flight to San Francisco and the wedding of my niece Beth, a gifted clarinetist with auburn hair, sparkling blue eyes, and an infectious, refreshing laugh.

Beth and her fiancé, James, had visited Mom last summer at her cottage under the Bridge and, aside from being awarded a speeding ticket just west of St. Ignace, James had made a favorable impression.

So favorable, in fact, that the entire family—Mom, her four children, and a tribe of grandchildren—arranged to meet in San Francisco for the nuptials, underwritten by my nephew David, the thirty-year-old retired Microsoft millionaire, now devoting his young life to swing dancing.

What could I offer the struggling newlyweds that young David couldn't, I thought? A lesson in square-dancing?

I pondered for a long time, and then slapped myself. "Eureka!" I exclaimed, as the California gold miners were said to have shouted when they struck the mother lode. Roughly translated, it means "I have found it!" (What, I wondered, is the Greek word for the phrase, "I have lost it"?)

In any case, and especially in this case, the mother lode would be a few fillets of fresh whitefish, iced down and topped with several pounds of shiny, freshly picked sweet cherries. Now, that would be a regal treasure that brilliant young David could only pixilate and hardly duplicate.

Excited at the prospect of being a celebrity among celebrities, I stopped at John Cross Fisheries and, on the advice of the friendly young clerk, emptied my camera bag to provide the perfect travel container for 2.55 pounds of beautifully wrapped whitefish, sandwiched between two pounds of frozen gel.

Further down the road I stopped at a roadside stand and added five pounds of firm, translucent cherries—yes, plucked that very day!—to the cool bundle. Naturally, in doing this, I checked the fish, tapping them gently to make sure they were healthy and enjoying a restful trip. They nodded lazily and fell back to sleep.

During the final leg to the airport, I imagined the newly-weds, honeymooning among the Redwoods of northern California, pitching a tent and popping sweet, juicy Michigan cherries into each other's mouths while awaiting their whitefish feast that was slowly simmering on the grill.

At security, I asked that the honeymoon treasure be hand inspected, lest any harm be done by those infernally invasive X-rays.

Eight hours later, I was warmly greeted by sister, Cilla, her husband, Sandy, and Mom at their plush time-share—an 18th-floor penthouse in central San Francisco, a gift of Sandy's sister. As delightful as the accommodations were, my only concern was: did they have a refrigerator?

Double Eureka! Luck was still on my side, and I quickly removed the fish from the travel case, tapped the tender trio, and stashed them under the icemaker. Mission accomplished. And now, the moment to announce the grand scheme was at hand.

"That my dear family," pointing to the fridge with a

swagger of unconcealed delight, "is the treasure of Michigan's North—plump fresh whitefish a la cherries divine! A wedding feast nonpareil! Toss everything else overboard!"

There was a respectful moment of silence, then my sister intoned quietly, touching my shoulder ever so gently: "But Freddie, don't you remember that Beth and James are VEGETARIANS?" She paused for effect. "And *strict* vegetarians, at that? They won't TOUCH the whitefish, and the very thought of it will probably make them sick!"

"But," she added with great sympathy, "I know they'll LOVE the cherries."

You can imagine, I think, how completely crushed I felt. Cherries without whitefish? Love without marriage? The platitudes of life raced through my mind. "Life is unfair," John F. Kennedy told most of the rest of the world. "No good deed shall go unpunished," said someone less profound.

That wasn't the end of the whitefish, however. The newly-to-be-weds had thoughtfully chosen to invite friends and relatives to the rehearsal dinner, to be held in Santa Rosa north of the Golden Gate Bridge—but only those between the ages of twenty and forty.

This neatly excluded all but one of the sixteen-member Gray entourage, with only young David making the cut. It also neatly packaged the whitefish lovers, who spent a good part of the next day orchestrating our own evening celebration of sixty years of family tales set in the Michigan North. And indeed, it turned out to be a most memorable occasion.

For there, among the towering eucalyptus of the Mills College campus, for one sweet fragrant summer evening, family was fortune, and Lake Michigan whitefish was king.

UP A RIVER WITHOUT A PADDLE

Without a car, northern michigan can be an archipelago of sparsely inhabited islands in a sea of swampland. A murky metaphor, perhaps, but that's exactly where I found myself early one June morning, marooned at Dave's Auto Repair Shop as a direct consequence of having tempted fate.

I had calculated I would save hundreds of dollars by having the ball joints on my 1994 Ford Explorer replaced by a skilled and honest mechanic, the one who only months earlier had breathed new life into my trusty, if aging, steed for under one hundred dollars.

Dave had taken my word on the ball joints, just as I had taken the word of a well-meaning local mechanic.

But, once Dave put the car up on the jack, he told me the good news—the ball joints were fine. And the bad news— my Explorer needed new brakes, a U-joint, and some other work. Dave said he'd have to order a part that wouldn't get in until about 2:00 p.m. Still, he assured me, he would have the car ready for me by 5:00 p.m.

I did some quick calculations and realized that even if Dave did his usual diligent work, I'd either lose a day's wages or have to take a cab to and from Petoskey, at roughly $100 round trip. I slapped myself in despair.

Not a great choice, especially since I was saving every penny for a root canal followed by a week's vacation in the great Canadian north to recover. I faced the possibility that one of the two, or both, would have to be sacrificed.

Then, I remembered I had written an article about the Straits Regional Ride bus service that had begun two years ago to provide public transportation in four counties, including trips between Cheboygan and Petoskey. The initial scheduled routes had been replaced by on-call service and, although it was intended primarily for the elderly and the disabled, I figured that at this point in my life I qualified as both and would take advantage of the opportunity, if it presented itself.

I explained my dilemma to Dave and asked him to hold up on ordering the parts while I called the bus dispatcher.

I tried to find the number in Dave's greasy phone book but there was no entry under Straits Regional Ride, so I concluded it had succumbed to a lack of interest. (Only later did I learn that the entry was listed under "Straights" Regional Ride, two inches above where it would be had it been spelled correctly!)

Just as Dave gave me the card of the local taxi driver, I recalled that the bus service was effectively underwritten by what was then known as Crossroads Services, to transport its employees to and from work each day at a fixed fee. I gave Crossroads a call and was given the number of the dispatcher, who chirped those golden words: "Not a problem. We have a bus leaving for Petoskey in fifteen minutes. We'll pick up you up."

"What is the fare?" I asked timidly, stroking the single ten dollar bill in my wallet.

"Three dollars each way," she responded, sending me halfway to Wawa with delight.

When 9:00 a.m. turned into 10:00 a.m. with no sign of a bus, I phoned the dispatcher.

"Thank goodness you called," she said. "The driver thought he was to pick up at Dave's in Indian River, but now he's headed back to Cheboygan and will be there in a few minutes. Don't move."

You can imagine my relief when that shiny white bus with blue lettering pulled into the parking lot and the front entry door folded against itself, inviting me in.

There was one seat left, at the rear of the bus. I handed the driver my ten dollar bill and tucked away the seven singles in change for the return trip.

I was absolutely elated at my good fortune, and chatted with the elderly passengers about the delights of public transportation in the Michigan north.

The driver dropped me off at the News-Review, and picked me up five hours later for the return trip, again in a fully loaded bus.

As I picked up my newly repaired car, I realized I had tasted what it feels like to be marooned on an island and to be saved by the fleeting recollection of a service that might have made good newspaper copy but was far from reality for me—until it became a necessity.

I encourage you to learn to misspell *Straits* as *Straights* should you ever find yourself up a similar river without a paddle.

STRANDED

My little horse must think it queer
To stop without a farmhouse near
Between the woods and frozen lake
The darkest evening of the year.
"Stopping by Woods," by Robert Frost

L IKE ROBERT FROST, I HAD STOPPED BY WOODS ON A SNOWY
evening. And I shared the poet's melancholy when I
realized that, following a profoundly inept maneuver,
the rear of my decade-old Explorer had become fatally
engaged in a snow bank along this untraveled road.

There I was, immobile at midnight, a few miles from
home, and I knew there would be no travelers at that late
hour to offer assistance.

Clumps of snow fell like large, wet cotton balls,
enshrouding me in my warm metal tomb; and, no amount of
frenzied spinning of wheels would set me free.

I had spent the previous few hours in the luxury of an
Eddie Bauer SUV, driven through light snow by brother, Bill,
with Mom, his wife, Carol, and me as passengers, on a
return trip from Grand Rapids after a funeral service for my
Uncle Howard.

After picking up my car in town and driving north, alone, along M-119, a lake-effect storm sought me out and delivered a full frontal assault on the slopes between the woods and the frozen lake. I felt I had been caught in an avalanche.

I chastised myself for thinking my aging companion, long of tooth and short of tread, could successfully climb the long and winding road. A more sensible person would have taken a less challenging route.

I had worked my way well up the mile-long slope, but when I was within yards of the crest of the hill, my trusty steed of 300,000 miles would go no further, despite a fully functioning tachometer.

I opened the door, wrenched myself around in the seat and peered behind, determined to retrace my path back to the main road. But, the rapidly falling snow had already covered my tracks and I had to feel my way cautiously over the thick blanket of snow.

When I was close to my target, the intersection of State and Robinson roads, I mistook a set of depressions in the snow for my tire tracks and, with a final surge of confidence, backed soundly into the snow bank.

In despair at the hour and desolation, I checked my hubs to make certain they were locked. Believing I was in four-wheel drive, I raced the engine, but to no avail. As there was nothing further to do, I wrapped myself in the blankets I carried for emergencies, shut off the engine, and resigned myself to spending a long winter night in the woods.

After a fitful hour of sleep, the headlights of an approaching pickup returned me to consciousness. A couple, returning from a party, offered their help; but the towrope they normally carried was missing and their cellular phone could not find a signal.

They dropped me off at the home of Joe Davis, a mechanic down the road, where a lamp glowed in a window. Joe appeared at the door, dressed in his pajamas, and offered to help.

After quickly donning his work clothes, Joe pulled my Explorer from the snow with his wrecker and hauled me over the crest of the hill, leaving me to find my way home.

Many a sorry adventure such as mine has its silver linings, and in this case there were two.

When I related my story to our local road commissioners they puzzled over the inability of my Explorer to make its way out of the snow bank using its four-wheel drive. After a few questions, they surmised I had failed to engage the system by not pushing a now-obvious button on the dashboard. That proved to be the secret and I was able to make it up Robinson Road and other challenging ones throughout the rest of the winter.

The commissioners soothed the sting I suffered from having to admit my own incompetence, by complimenting me for staying with my vehicle, rather than wandering off in search of help.

And, last week, on the occasion of my sixty-second birthday, brother Bill gifted me with a cellular phone, complete with five hundred minutes of air time. "We don't want to lose you," he said.

Nor do I, I thought, wondering what new trouble I could safely get into—and out of.

THE PIANO TUNER

THE PIANO TUNER FROM GAYLORD AGREED TO MEET ME AT Audie's in Mackinaw City. The idea was to rendezvous at a known location and travel together to Cilla's cottage, a quarter-mile away in Wawatam Beach, where he would administer the Baldwin's first tune-up in seven years.

It turned out that Bill, the piano man whom I had never met, spent half an hour in the parking lot behind the restaurant looking for me while I turned circles in front in despair, peering in every moving and parked vehicle, looking for Bill, afraid we had missed each other.

Why did I think I'd recognize Bill at first sight? Don't all piano tuners look alike? Plus, I'd heard his voice over the phone. Weren't those clues enough?

Though I was ten minutes late—blame it on roadway construction—I hardly thought Bill would abandon the chance for his second musical gig of the day. An hour earlier he had tuned the family's parlor grand at my brother's house in Alanson and called me from there.

Most importantly though, he hadn't yet been paid.

In that half hour, I thrice went back to the cottage, opened it up, checked for signs of forced entry (Bill had the address), played a few chords on the spinet to make sure it was still sour, and then, painfully assured that it was, locked up and returned to Audie's.

This third time back, I saw a middle-aged guy on the corner, hunkered in a jacket, looking confused and bewildered.

I waved to him. "You Bill?"

He nodded and approached my car.

"Been waiting long?" I said.

"About half an hour," he grimaced, pointing to the back parking lot.

I didn't have the heart to ask why in blazes he waited for me there. Did I sound like I regularly met guys in back parking lots?

But, he turned out to be a fine piano man and, in fact, played with the trumpet player friend of mine, Dan Jacobs of Bellaire, whose group enjoys considerable national renown.

An hour later, Bill spread his wings and gave me thirty seconds of Dixieland stride before turning on the bench to let me know he thought highly of the instrument. He also showed me the innards, where the previous tuner had signed his name seven years ago; then Bill added his own.

His final suggestion: tuning a piano once a year was more in keeping with accepted standards, although he allowed that leaving it in the unheated cottage over the winter was excellent therapy.

AND THE BEETS GO ON

IT ALL BEGAN WITH A HALF BUSHEL OF BEETS WITHOUT greens offered at $6.95 at Bill's Farm Market on a fine autumn day several weeks ago. Usually beets with greens, if you can find them, sell for about $1 for a bunch of three, so I figured buying the two hundred beets that Mom counted had saved me $193.05.

Even if Mom had miscounted, say by half, I had saved a bundle. So, I invested the surplus in the remaining ingredients for Borscht Moscovskaya, my favorite soup named after the Russian capital, and the highlight, incidentally, of the restaurant scene in the film *Dr. Zhivago*, where the rogue Viktor Komarovsky was bent on seducing the beautiful Lara.

The soup has always worked for me, gastronomically at least, and every six months or so I boil up a steaming cauldron, wolf down about half over the course of a week—each bowl laced with sour cream and fresh dill—and freeze the rest for gifts and midnight snacks.

So, last Saturday I packed the backseat of the car with the ingredients for several tureens worth of borscht, and invited Mom to accompany me to the cottage in Mackinaw City under the Bridge for a final afternoon of raking leaves, futzing about in the kitchen, and watching wildlife in the backyard before sealing up our favorite retreat for the winter.

I told Mom, now ninety-two, that she need not help the mound of beets that rose from the sink, like the oven from a volcano; but she insisted. I propped her up on a kitchen stool and off we went. Mom peeled while I slice each beet into 1/8-inch thick by two-inch long strips.

As with "Ninety-nine Bottles of Beer on the Wall," the song that never ends, Mom counted the beets remaining in the sink as she worked, which only made me aware of the painful process that would drag on for hours. And it became even more painful when Mom sliced her finger and we had to scurry to find a bandage.

During our afternoon of peeling, Mom laughingly recounted the anguish she suffered whenever we kids trudged merrily through the kitchen door with yet another bushel of peaches for her to pickle and jar.

Best of all was carrying the filled Mason jars to the root cellar and neatly placing them on unlit wooden shelves where they were kept cool by the dark soil floor and whitewashed stone walls.

I can still taste the cinnamon and cloves in the pickling.

And, as with Borscht Moscovskaya, the total experience—the picking, peeling, the preparation—lingers in my memory like a fine perfume.

ABOUT THE AUTHOR

FRED GRAY IS CURRENTLY DIRECTOR OF INFORMATION and Website Development for Emmet County, Michigan (www.emmetcounty.org). He also owns and operates his personal website, www.flowingwellproductions.com, where you can purchase additional copies of *That's Outrageous!* and photography.